WELSH MARCHES POMONA

MICHAEL PORTER

WELSH MARCHES POMONA

ILLUSTRATED BY MARGARET A. V. GILL

MARCHER APPLE NETWORK

Published by Marcher Apple Network, MMX

© MMX Marcher Apple Network

ISBN 978 0 9555621 3 6

Printed in Wales by Gomer Press

Designed by Wayne Summers

This book is dedicated to everybody who has brought us apples to identify

ACKNOWLEDGEMENTS

THE author wishes to thank all who have contributed in any way to the compilation of this book: foremost, I am grateful to the artist, Margaret Gill, whose patience and expertise has resulted in such accurate and beautiful illustrations.

Present or former members of staff at the National Fruit Collections at Brogdale, particularly Emma-Jane Allen, Alison Lean, Joan Morgan, Matthew Ordidge, Pippa Palmer and Mary Pennell, provided considerable help in identification of apple varieties and information about accessions, as well as sending samples of blossom and fruit for research and illustration.

Jim Arbery of the Royal Horticultural Society and staff at the Lindley Library provided help and guidance in the research of several varieties.

The National Orchard Forum has given encouragement and support throughout the project.

Members of the Gloucestershire Orchard Group, particularly Alan Watson and Charles Martell, were helpful in locating specimens for study.

Members of staff at the Shropshire Record Office, Hereford City Library, the Elgar Museum at Broadheath and Hereford Cider Museum have all been generous with their help in tracing the history of certain varieties of apples.

Nick Dunn of Frank P. Matthews and Chris Fairs of H. P. Bulmer Ltd. gave practical help by providing information and specimens for examination. James Bissett of Herefordshire Council assisted with several aspects of publicity. Gerard Greenen of Plant Cytometry Services analysed the ploidy level of various cultivars.

John Aldridge was a ready source of information throughout the project; he re-found NEWLAND SACK and grafted many of the first trees to be planted in the Museum Orchards of the Marcher Apple Network (MAN). For several years Paul Davis has propagated unusual varieties for our collections and he provided information about the local Welsh apples. John Savidge has helped with the identification of local varieties.

Several members of MAN have carried out research into local varieties included in this Pomona and generously shared their information with us. Peter Weeks researched CHATLEY KERNEL; Muriel Beck traced the history of BRITHMAWR; Ray Jeavon showed us ONIBURY PIPPIN; Charles Martell unmasked the true TEN COMMANDMENTS of Hogg, though David Jones,

Dennis Gwatkin and Chris Fairs also took an active part in the quest. Graham Sprackling helped to map the distribution of LANDORE in Herefordshire and Mr. and Mrs. Gaine showed us the Landore trees around Craswall and Michaelchurch Escley.

Many of the varieties illustrated in the book were cultivated in our museum orchards at Tredomen, Llangynidr and Westhope and we thank the owners of these orchards for their unstinting support. Specimens were also provided by the National Trust from the collection of local apples established at Berrington Hall by Stanley Baldock for the National Council for the Conservation of Plants and Gardens; we are very grateful to the Head Gardener, Nick Winney, for all his help.

We wish to thank the following who allowed us to visit their orchards and collect fruit for research: John Bunn (Checkley), Colin and Daphne Gardener (Llangenny), Sir Andrew Large (Cui Parc), David Millar (Llyswen), Ivor and Brian Morris (Aston-on-Clun), Mrs. C. M. Rawlings (Swainshill), Mrs. M Richardson (Llyswen), John Tedstone (Eardisland), Mr. and Mrs. T. Thomas (Llanwrda), Diana Uhlman (Croft Castle), Mr. and Mrs. Malcolm Watkins (Clytha). Mr. and Mrs. Gordon Batchelor told us about Frank Whiting's fruit farm at Credenhill.

Many visitors who brought fruit for identification at apple shows such as *The Big Apple* at Much Marcle, Malvern Autumn Fruit Show and the apple fairs at Leominster and Church Stretton have contributed to our knowledge of local apples. At such events surprises emerge from unlikely places, such as the GIPSY KING trio extracted from the satchel of Tom Adams at Church Stretton and the clutch of small BARCELONA PEARMAINS which Mary Troughton pulled out of a brown paper bag at Malvern.

I am most appreciative of the help and guidance provided by Wayne Summers who was responsible for graphic design and Pit Dafis of Gomer Press for overseeing production of the book.

Finally, I am very grateful to my fellow enthusiasts in MAN who formed the Pomona Committee: Peter Austerfield (Chairman), Ray Boddington, Celia Kirby, Sheila Leitch, Sylvia O'Brien, Chris Porter and Richard Wheeler, who provided encouragement and support throughout the enterprise.

CONTENTS

LIST OF PLATES

FOREWORD

BY SIR ANDREW LARGE, PRESIDENT OF THE MARCHER APPLE NETWORK

SINCE 1993, when a group of enthusiasts created the Marcher Apple Network, its members have worked to protect traditional orchards and prevent the extinction of many varieties of apples once grown in the Welsh Marches. The determined effort of the group is rekindling an interest in the wonderful range of fruit which we inherited.

The Welsh Marches is an area of fascinating diversity: from the relatively warm, dry regions in the lower Wye and Severn valleys, sheltered from the west winds by the Welsh mountains, to the damper hill country and wide views of the Brecon Beacons. The apples which grow there reflect this diversity.

In earlier times, particularly in the 19th century, Herefordshire and its surrounding counties was the cradle of a huge fruit-growing area and every farm and settlement either had its own orchards, yielding fruit for sale or domestic consumption, or would enjoy the produce of the travelling cider mills which frequented the region. Fruit and trees of such varied nature: colour, size, shape, texture, aroma, flavour: the diversity was truly remarkable. Unfortunately, over the last hundred years or so, much of this heritage was lost. But the enthusiastic members of MAN have searched in many corners of the area; from private gardens to derelict orchards on remote hillsides or in the shadow of long abandoned farms; bit by bit this heritage has been rediscovered and the fruits and trees preserved for future generations.

This is a locally inspired book. The apples described originated in the Welsh Marches and include old varieties rediscovered in local orchards. Written by Michael Porter, an eminent botanist and pomologist, and illustrated by Margaret Gill, an accomplished artist and botanical illustrator, the *Pomona* has been painstakingly researched over several years.

Thanks to that diligence we now have this wonderful book in which some of our local apples are described and illustrated for the first time. And hopefully this book will give pleasure way beyond the Marches, as more and more groups of enthusiasts around our country rediscover the delights and variety of long-forgotten fruit.

INTRODUCTION

1 THE AREA

THE region known as the Welsh Marches as used in the title refers to the borderland of England and Wales which is home to The Marcher Apple Network (MAN). Our area extends from the southern boundary of Cheshire to the Bristol Channel and includes the counties on both sides of Offa's Dyke. In Norman times it was a fluctuating buffer zone between England and Wales occupied by the largely autonomous Marcher Lordships and, before the administrative reforms of the Tudors, its extent and position at any particular time was difficult to ascertain. Several travel writers have explored the region: *In the March and Borderland of Wales*, A. G. Bradley (1908), *Highways and Byways in the Welsh Marches*, S. P. B. Mais (1939), *Welsh Border Country*, P. Thoresby Jones (1939) and *The Southern Marches*, H. J. Massingham (1952) all provide informative, though sometimes controversial, accounts of this beautiful countryside as it was in the early part of the twentieth century.

The domestic or sweet apple (*Malus pumila*) has been cultivated in this territory for centuries. The wild crab apple (*Malus sylvestris*) is an uncommon native woodland tree, often difficult to distinguish from the widespread seedling offspring of domestic apples which have sprung up from discarded cores in hedges and copses. Welsh laws attributed to Hywel Dda, king of most of Wales in the tenth century, placed a price of sixty pence on a fruiting sweet apple tree, accounting it equal in value to a cow and half as valuable as an oak tree. A crab apple tree was valued at thirty pence.

In a charter issued by Harold, Lord of Ewias, recording a grant he made to the Priory of Ewias when it was founded in 1100, apples are listed as one of the crops grown on his castle demesne; they are also recorded in 1175 in a grant of tithes to Brecon Priory made by Roger, Lord of Tretower (Ystradyw). At this period apples were mainly cultivated in the well-protected orchards of castles and religious houses. By the fourteenth century leases in the archives of the Beaufort Estate record small orchards on burgage plots in Monmouth. In 1359 apples and other fruit valued at half a mark (six shillings and eightpence) are noted in the tithes of the Vicar of Ewias Harold, in Herefordshire.

CIDER ORCHARDS

From the sixteenth century, in more peaceful times in the Marches, the planting of orchards gained pace. A map of Tretower, near Crickhowell, in a manorial survey of 1587, shows an orchard of about ten acres called Perllan y Castell adjacent to the castle green and at some time during the sixteenth century a cider cellar was built at Tretower Court. Cider cellars became standard features of the larger farmhouses in this area, built during the sixteenth and seventeenth centuries as cider became an important element in the agricultural economy. A comment from the herbalist John Gerard, quoted in *The Herefordshire Pomona*, indicates that there were extensive cider apple orchards around Hereford in 1597, and in 1629 John Parkinson writes that a large quantity of the cider made in the west of England was being supplied to ships undertaking long sea voyages. At this time GENNET MOYLE was reputed to be the favourite cider apple variety, particularly in that part of Monmouthshire and west Herefordshire known as Archenfield. GENNET MOYLE was supplanted by the famous REDSTREAK, renowned for the fine flavour of its cider, probably introduced by Lord Scudamore of Holme Lacy early in the seventeenth century. His considerable influence persuaded many landowners that orchards were a sound investment and these were planted with such enthusiasm that John Evelyn comments in the preface to his *Pomona* (1664) "all Herefordshire is become, in a manner, but one entire orchard."

However, the profitability of cider orchards waxed and waned, being affected by various factors such as the introduction of a tax on cider and increased competition from beer and imported wines. At the end of the eighteenth century orchards were in decline and Thomas Andrew Knight, author of *Pomona Herefordiensis*, considered many of the old varieties of cider apple, such as REDSTREAK, "to be affected by the debilitated old age of variety". This idea stimulated him to breed new varieties such as DOWNTON PIPPIN and the FOXLEY APPLE as replacements for what he considered to be the effete old sorts. Later in the nineteenth century the flood of imported apples from North America threatened the survival of British fruit growers. Meeting this challenge was one of the factors which prompted the compilation of *The Herefordshire Pomona* by the

Woolhope Naturalists' Field Club as part of their effort to improve the management of local orchards. Local nurseries were commissioned to produce large stocks of some of the best sorts of cider apple and Knight's view on the limited life of varieties was largely disproved when hundreds of vigorous young trees of old varieties such as FOXWHELP, SKYRME'S KERNEL and HAGLOE CRAB were distributed among club members and planted in orchards throughout Herefordshire. Perhaps the success of their venture can be gauged by the fact that, between 1870 and 1900, no fewer than 12 cider making factories opened around Hereford (Morgan and Richards, 1993).

The three counties of Gloucestershire, Herefordshire and Worcestershire are at the heart of an important fruit-growing area which has long been famous for its orchards. One hundred years ago almost every farm and smallholding maintained an orchard, often with a range of fruit from apples and pears to plums, damsons and cherries. Many smallholders cultivated a wide range of varieties, carefully selected to provide ripe produce for the local market throughout the autumn, winter and spring. Even small cottages boasted a few fruit trees which made a significant contribution to the domestic economy. Larger commercial orchards supplied fruit by rail to the urban populations in distant towns, or sent cider apples and perry pears to the cider manufacturers.

In 1899, when the nurseryman John Basham described conditions in Monmouthshire orchards in a paper for the Royal Horticultural Society, there were 230,000 acres (95,000 hectares) of orchards in the United Kingdom, of which roughly 30% were in the Welsh Marches. Nearly all were traditional orchards of standard trees. During the twentieth century, particularly after the Second World War, there was a dramatic decline in the area under orchard cultivation. Changes in farming practice, together with other factors such as the rise of supermarkets, rendered orchards of large standard trees uneconomical. In the latter part of the last century, until 1993, incentive payments were available to farmers for grubbing out orchards and by the end of the century there were less than 62,000 acres (25,000 hectares) left in the United Kingdom. Not only had the total area under orchard cultivation fallen dramatically, but its nature had utterly changed: nearly all the orchards John Basham visited in 1899 were traditional ones composed of standard trees; by 2000, nearly all were commercial orchards of intensively managed small trees. It has been estimated that over 95% of our traditional orchards disappeared during the twentieth century.

DECLINE IN TRADITIONAL ORCHARDS AND THE RANGE OF APPLES GROWN

The few remaining standard orchards are mainly planted with cider apple varieties and situated in the best growing areas, often close to cider works. In less favourable areas for fruit production, further west on higher ground with less fertile soils, only remnants of farm orchards remain, sometimes consisting of just a few decrepit old trees. All orchards enhance the biodiversity of the countryside but traditional orchards, particularly old ones which are not intensively managed, offer the greatest benefits for associated wildlife, providing habitats for epiphytes such as mosses and lichens and the semi-parasitic mistletoe, and nesting sites for birds like redstarts, nuthatches and mistle thrushes. Standard trees live longer and can therefore provide greater continuity of habitat.

Almost 400 years ago the practical Yorkshire gardener William Lawson expressed his delight in sharing his orchard with "a brood of nightingales", not only for their song which kept him company night and day, but also for their help in ridding his fruit trees of "Caterpillars, and all noisome worms and flies". Having almost disappeared, traditional orchards are at last being recognised as important for biodiversity. As well as being havens for wildlife these ancient orchards may also be the last refuge of varieties of fruit which have totally disappeared from general cultivation. In the last ten years several old apples which are not even represented in the National Fruit Collections at Brogdale, such as BARCELONA PEARMAIN and BRINGEWOOD PIPPIN, have been re-found in old farm orchards in the Welsh Marches. There are advantages in conserving local varieties of cultivated plants which may be well adapted to local conditions, as well as possessing other attributes such as the distinctive aroma and flavour of a SUMMER QUOINING. The upsurge in the number of orchard groups established during the past ten years indicates an increasing awareness of orchards for a host of reasons, including the provision of local food.

During the last century, the decline in extent of orchards was accompanied by a fall in the number of varieties of apple in cultivation. At the turn of the twentieth century, Frank Whiting, who had a small fruit farm in the village of Credenhill near Hereford, cultivated about 170 sorts of dessert and culinary apples, including several local ones such as CHATLEY KERNEL and CREDENHILL PIPPIN. He supplied apples by train to markets as far afield as Edinburgh. About the same time local nurseries such as King's Acre Nurseries, Hereford, and Richard Smith and Sons, Worcester, listed in their catalogues as many as 200 varieties of apple. More than 260 dessert and culinary apples and upwards of 140 cider varieties are reputed to have originated in the Welsh Marches. About 48% of the former are still grown, mainly in special collections, but a smaller proportion of the cider varieties remain in cultivation.

TRADITION OF LOCAL POMONAS

Many of the old fruit varieties are described and beautifully illustrated in early pomonas associated with the Welsh Marches. Thomas Andrew Knight, of Downton Castle, the newly-elected President of the London Horticultural Society, compiled the *Pomona Herefordiensis*, which was issued in parts and published by the Agricultural Society of Herefordshire in 1811. This contains descriptions of 30 varieties of cider apple and perry pear, ranging from old local cider apples like THE FRIAR and PAWSAN to new varieties raised by Knight, such as DOWNTON PIPPIN and GRANGE APPLE. Twenty-seven of the fruit were illustrated by Miss Elizabeth Matthews and three by Knight's eldest daughter Frances. The plates were engraved by William Hooker.

The Herefordshire Pomona, issued in seven parts between 1878 and 1884, and published in two volumes in 1885, contains descriptions and illustrations of 432 apples and pears. Originally it was intended to restrict the work to Herefordshire fruit, but the project was extended to embrace "The principal Apples and Pears which are grown in various parts of the country." This magnificent work was published by the Woolhope Naturalists' Field Club of Hereford and jointly edited by their leading light, Dr. Henry Graves Bull and the foremost British pomologist, Dr. Robert Hogg. The illustrations, which are an outstanding feature, were reproduced by chromolithography from watercolour paintings by Miss Alice Blanche Ellis and Edith Elizabeth, eldest daughter of Dr. Bull. The original watercolour paintings, including some which were not published in *The Herefordshire Pomona*, are on permanent exhibition at the Cider Museum in Hereford.

Bulmer's Pomona was published in 1987 to mark the centenary of the cider maker H. P. Bulmer Ltd. Thirty-five varieties of cider apple, considered to be the most important introduced during the previous 100 years, are described by the eminent pomologist Ray Williams, and illustrated in watercolour by Caroline Todhunter.

All three books are valuable aids for the identification of local apples and pears and *Welsh Marches Pomona* aims to supplement this series by providing descriptions and illustrations of some of the local varieties of apples which were not fully covered in the illustrious works listed above.

2 ABOUT THE BOOK

SELECTION OF VARIETIES

Welsh Marches Pomona contains descriptions and illustrations of thirty-one dessert and culinary apples of local provenance which have not been fully described in earlier publications. The selection includes varieties introduced since 1885, such as KING'S ACRE BOUNTIFUL and BYFORD WONDER and also some which have little or no written history like MARGED NICOLAS, PIG YR WYDD and GREEN PURNELL. The majority of varieties described are known to have been cultivated in Victorian times, but somehow escaped the clutches of the editors of *The Herefordshire Pomona*. In several cases, for example SWEENEY NONPAREIL and TEWKESBURY BARON, written descriptions can be found in old apple handbooks, notably *The Fruit Manual* (fifth edition, 1884) by Robert Hogg, but these accounts are not illustrated. A small number, including BRIDSTOW WASP and SEVERN BANK featured in watercolour paintings prepared for *The Herefordshire Pomona* but were not included in the published work. In two or three instances, varieties which appear in *The Herefordshire Pomona* are also included in *Welsh Marches Pomona* because at some time in the past there has been debate about their identity.

DESCRIPTIONS

Variety descriptions are mainly based on a study of standard and half-standard trees growing in orchards in the Welsh Marches. There have been comparisons with older trees in farm orchards in this area and with trees in the National Fruit Collections at Brogdale.

At least 15 apples of each variety were examined and measured and that information entered on a Recording Sheet (see page 18). This is a modified version of one developed by Wye College and Brogdale Horticultural Trust during their project to develop a UK Network for Malus. The descriptive terms used are defined in a Glossary (see pages 82 *et seq.*). The information was collected over three years to give some impression of variation caused by environmental factors. The results were used to compose the descriptions which accompany each entry.

For each variety there is a short account of its history and any other relevant information; although identifica-tion of varieties is mainly based on fruits, additional details relating to other characters are included as these may be further aids to identification.

ILLUSTRATIONS

Beneath the text are line drawings showing a longitudinal section (left) and transverse section (right) of a ripe fruit. On the page opposite the text there are watercolour paintings of at least two ripe fruit, with different views showing details of their external morphology. A sprig of blossom is also illustrated. Fruit, blossoms and sections are all shown life-size.

Leaf morphology is shown in line drawings on pages 90 & 91; in all cases the leaves were collected in late summer from a position midway along a new lateral shoot.

VARIATION

The fact that all living organisms show variation was one of the observations on which Charles Darwin built his explanation of Natural Selection as a force bringing about evolution. From observation of thousands of apples brought to fruit shows and other apple events for identification, it has become clear that varieties show a greater degree of variation than is generally admitted in the literature, and this is one of the main stumbling blocks in the process of identification. Named varieties of apple are propagated vegetatively in order to maintain their characteristic features. Trees raised from seeds will incorporate features from both parents and therefore not exactly match any particular variety, though they may occasionally provide the basis for a new one. Environmental and genetic factors both contribute to the variation shown by individuals. Old varieties of apple like BLENHEIM ORANGE and KING OF THE PIPPINS tend to show the greatest degree of genetic variation, possibly because seedlings similar to the parent have broadened our concept of that variety.

Environmental factors, such as the amount of sunshine or rainfall experienced, may alter the amount of russet on varieties such as FORESTER or LEATHERCOAT RUSSET, so that in some years the apples will be extensively russeted and in other years there will be little or no russet. Even fruits growing on different parts of the same tree will differ according to the amount of light available to them. But, whereas only changes in the genotype can be transmitted to offspring and potentially be instrumental in bringing about evolution, both sorts of variation can make identification more difficult. Both sorts of variation can also undermine the reliability of identification keys in which the outcome is determined by a small number of characters. Flower and fruit characters are generally considered to be more constant than vegetative ones, but even these show variation. In an analytical key for the identification of varieties in *The Fruit Manual*, Robert Hogg uses the three positions of the stamens in the tube (see glossary) as the first dividing point, indicating that he considered this to be a constant feature. However, in his introduction he warns "I have adopted them as the primary divisions of this system, having found by experience that they are on the whole the most reliable characters where all are more or less changeable."

If an artificial key has been used for identification, it is essential to check the outcome carefully against a detailed description of the variety.

SYNONYMS AND OTHER NOMENCLATURE COMPLICATIONS

A variety may be known under different names in different places. This is another circumstance which can lead to confusion and the misidentification of varieties.

According to Hogg (1884), POMEROY OF HEREFORD-SHIRE was also known as KIRKE'S FAME, PEACH, SUSSEX PEACH and RUSSET PINE. Smith (1971) notes that, in the National Fruit Collections, where the variety is known as SUSSEX PEACH, it is "morphologically indistinguishable from PINE APPLE RUSSET OF DEVON". Around the village of Checkley in Herefordshire it is called SUGAR APPLE.

The conundrums caused by variation, compounded by the use of synonyms, come together to cause confusion in the identification of SAM'S CRAB. The variety was generally known as LONGVILLE'S KERNEL by pomologists in the early nineteenth century, but according to *The Herefordshire Pomona*, SAM'S CRAB was the name used by local people. However the situation was then complicated by conflicting statements which occur in the description of the variety. Referring to variation in the flavour, *The Herefordshire Pomona* states "It requires a warm soil and sunny situation to bring its fruit to perfection. In unfavourable situations it could hardly be recognised as the same apple." Later in the account it is noted "There are undoubtedly two varieties of this apple, or, as was quaintly expressed by an admirer of the fruit 'There are two sorts of SAM'S CRAB: a basket full of one kind is eaten the same day, but the same basket full of the other kind lasts three or four days'." Hogg (1884) takes the matter a stage further by recognising two varieties to which he assigns almost identical descriptions: a dessert apple called LONGVILLE'S KERNEL and a cider apple called SAM'S CRAB. The only differences noted are that the former has a conical tube whereas the latter has a funnel-shaped tube and a more regular shape. SAM'S CRAB apples from different trees can vary greatly in flavour. Fruit from mature trees generally has the best taste, but climatic and soil factors also affect the flavour.

A comparable challenge is found where the same name is used for different sorts of apple; for example three rather similar varieties are known in the West Midlands as SEVERN BANK. This particular puzzle appears to have existed for more than 130 years as preliminary paintings for *The Herefordshire Pomona* illustrate two varieties with this name. For some reason, possibly debate over their identity, neither was included in the published work. We have selected the one found most frequently in local farm orchards, which closely matches Hogg's description and which is present as a cooking apple in the National Fruit Collections, where there is also a cider variety with the same name.

The most extreme case of this sort of nomenclative confusion encountered during compilation of *Welsh Marches Pomona* was that of TEN COMMANDMENTS. While trying to find apples which matched both the account in Hogg (1884) and a watercolour illustration intended for *The Herefordshire Pomona*, we were shown no fewer than seven varieties which were claimed to be TEN COMMANDMENTS. The main impostor was REINETTE ROUGE ETOILÉE which turned up in orchards in several parts of the Welsh Marches and further afield. In Shropshire, an apple similar to the Somerset form of TEN COMMANDMENTS was examined and in the Golden Valley of Herefordshire a type of

QUOINING is known locally as TEN COMMANDMENTS. Eventually the authentic apple was discovered in Gloucestershire, which is home to another local variety known as NINE OF DIAMONDS which appears morphologically indistinguishable from TEN COMMANDMENTS. There is a similar cultivar in the National Fruit Collections at Brogdale. Some of the varieties which can be confused with TEN COMMANDMENTS are illustrated on pages 16 and 17.

The main purpose in compiling *Welsh Marches Pomona* is to help in the identification of local apples not fully treated in previous publications. Detailed descriptions, including illustrations, are important in enabling identification of species and varieties, which is a necessary prerequisite for any conservation measure. At a time when there is a very lively interest in ecology and biodiversity, especially in the context of the local environment, it is hoped that this book will make a useful contribution by aiding projects to promote local biodiversity and the conservation of the special and distinctive nature of the Welsh Marches.

All the varieties described in *Welsh Marches Pomona* have been planted, as standard trees, in the new Paramor Orchard, established by the Marcher Apple Network near Crickhowell, in Powys.

'Bishops Castle Ten Commandments'

(a)

(a*i*)

(b)

(a*ii*)

Plate 1: *Flowers, fruit (a i & a ii) and transverse section of fruit (a) of un-named apple from Bishops Castle, Shropshire, which closely resemble the Somerset Ten Commandments.*

A transverse section of the true Ten Commandments (b) is shown for comparison.

Reinette Rouge Etoilée

Plate 2: *Flowers, fruit and transverse section of fruit of Reinette Rouge Etoilée,*
which is sometimes confusingly called Ten Commandments.

RECORDING SHEET

Used to collect data for compiling variety descriptions (see Introduction).

VARIETY DESCRIPTIONS	DATE
Variety name	
Shape	
Ridges	
Crowns	
Aroma	
Bloom/Scarf skin	
Ground colour	
Over colour type and %	
Russet: distribution/colour/%	
Skin surface: even/hammered	
Hairline	
Skin texture: smooth/rough/dry/waxy/greasy	
Lenticels: distribution/size/prominence	
Lenticel shape	
Lenticel: areolar/colour/russet	
Eye: size	
Eye: open/closed	
Sepal pose	
Basin form: smooth/ridged/puckered/beaded	
Basin width (see diagram)	
Basin depth	
Cavity form: smooth/russet/regular/uneven/grooved	
Russet: colour/distribution	
Cavity width (see diagram)	
Cavity depth	
L. S. size (diameter x height) mm	
Symmetry	
Tube: form/size	
Stamen position	
Flesh: colour/texture	
Flavour: aroma/acidity	
Core location	
Cell shape	
Core-line position	
Seeds: shape/colour/size	
Stalk: length/width/end form	
Stalk: length relative to base	
Stalk cavity form	
T. S. Outline (ribbing)	
Carpel arrangement: axile open/closed/abaxile	

DESCRIPTIONS & PLATES

BRIDSTOW WASP

Synonyms: *Wasp Apple, Carnation*

— Early culinary —

THE variety is described in Hogg (1884), but mistakenly called BIRDSTOW WASP. It is named after the village of Bridstow, near Ross-on-Wye in Herefordshire. The apple is accurately illustrated and correctly named in a watercolour painted in September 1881 for *The Herefordshire Pomona* but not included in the published work. Hogg explains that it has the synonym WASP APPLE "because these insects are so fond of it". He also draws attention to a feature which may not pass unnoticed by the wasps: "The skin is greasy when handled and leaves the apple scent on the hands".

Although known in recent times as CARNATION around Hay-on-Wye, it does not correspond to the variety of that name described in *The National Apple Register*.

BRIDSTOW WASP is a robust, triploid cultivar which grows quickly into a large, rather gaunt tree, which fruits well from an early age. The fruit is in season from late August until October. It cooks to a creamy-yellow purée with a good flavour.

Size	*Large (80 × 65mm)*		Cavity	*Fairly regular, rather narrow, lined with brown russet which may spread to base, with sometimes a narrow streak extending to eye*
Shape	*Flat-round to round, often asymmetrical, with blunt ribs ending in uneven crowns*			
Skin	*Pale yellow, with orange-red flush and broken red stripes, smooth, with extensive bloom when unripe but greasy when ripe; aromatic*		Stalk	*Stout, short, usually within cavity*
			Flesh	*White, soft, tender, sub-acid with a pleasant aroma*
Lenticels	*Generally inconspicuous, small, round, pale brown*		Tube	*Deep, funnel-shaped (10−12mm), sometimes extending to core; stamens median*
Basin	*Fairly wide, often ribbed, sometimes puckered or beaded*		Core	*Axile-open or sometimes abaxile, cells large, ovate or elliptical*
			Seeds	*Plump, rather short (6−7mm), acute or blunt, mid chestnut-brown*
Eye	*Closed, often appearing pinched, sepals connivent, with spreading tips*		Flowers	*Pollination group 3 (12)*

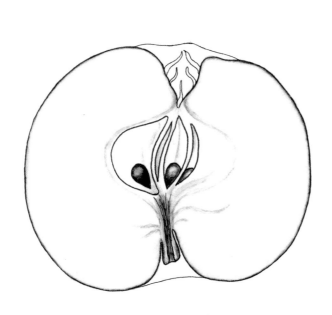

BRINGEWOOD PIPPIN

Late dessert or cider

THIS beautiful little apple was raised about 1800 by T. A. Knight of Downton Castle, Herefordshire, from a cross between GOLDEN PIPPIN and GOLDEN HARVEY. When elected as President of the Horticultural Society of London in 1811, Knight distributed scions of BRINDGEWOOD PIPPIN (*sic*) to members, writing "of this variety I have only seen a few Apples, which were very acid when taken from the tree, though apparently quite ripe, but became very excellent in February". He predicted that the variety "will prove very productive and valuable". Bringewood Chase is an area of woodland between Downton and Ludlow.

According to Hogg "The tree is hardy, but shows weak and slender growth and never attains a great size." He also records that Knight considered BRINGEWOOD PIPPIN a good cider apple. Having been apparently lost from cultivation for many years, an old tree of this variety was rediscovered in Shropshire in 2004. The fruit is in season from December until April.

Size	*Small (52 × 42mm)*	Cavity	*Regular, lined with fine greyish-brown russet*
Shape	*Round-conical, flattened at base and apex, regular*	Stalk	*Fairly sturdy, level with base or projecting*
Skin	*Smooth, dry, yellow, sometimes with a golden flush on sunny side, with fine pale greyish-brown russet around the apex and patchy russet radiating down the cheeks*	Flesh	*Creamy-yellow, firm texture, not very juicy, with a good contrast between sweetness and acidity*
		Tube	*Usually conical but sometimes a funnel with a short stem; stamens median or basal*
Lenticels	*Irregular, greyish-brown, difficult to differentiate from russet specks*	Core	*Small, median or basal, axile-closed, cells round or obovate*
Basin	*Fairly shallow, puckered or slightly beaded*	Seeds	*Broad, plump, (7–8mm)*
Eye	*Small, open, small sepals erect with spreading tips*	Flowers	*Pollination group 4 (14)*

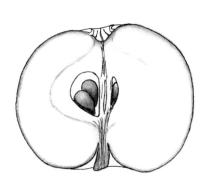
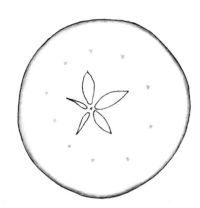

BRITHMAWR

Mid-season culinary

THE early history of this Welsh variety is unknown. It was exhibited by John Basham of Fairoak Nurseries, Bassaleg, Monmouthshire, at the Apples and Pears Conference held by the Royal Horticultural Society at the Crystal Palace in 1934. The last manager of Fairoak Nurseries, Joe Broom, confirmed the identity of the variety described here, which was found a few years ago in a garden near Cardiff. He commented that BRITHMAWR was still being sold by his nursery in the mid-twentieth century but was not a popular variety at that time.

The variety name refers to the fruit and translates as 'large speckled'.

Size	*Medium-large to large (75 × 62mm)*	Cavity	*Regular or occasionally lipped, lined with fine pale-brown russet which may streak out over the base*
Shape	*Round to oblong-conical, with blunt ribs ending in prominent crowns at apex*	Stalk	*Fairly long with rounded or flared tip; usually projecting beyond base*
Skin	*Smooth, pale yellowish-green, largely concealed by red stippling and broad splashes of dark red*	Flesh	*Cream, firm, fine-textured, juicy and sub-acid*
Lenticels	*Prominent as medium-sized, round or oval, grey dots*	Tube	*Long, narrow cone or slightly funnel-shaped; stamens marginal or median*
Basin	*Fairly deep, ribbed and sometimes puckered*	Core	*Usually axile-open, with broad obovate cells*
		Seeds	*Rather straight-sided and somewhat triangular (7–8mm)*
Eye	*Medium-large, usually partly open, sepals erect-convergent often with reflexed tips*	Flowers	*Pollination group 3 (11)*

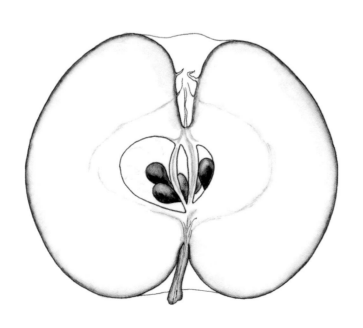

BROOKES'S

Late dessert

RECORDED in 1820 by the London Horticultural Society, this variety was said to be well known and much esteemed in Shropshire. It was grown in the gardens of the Royal Horticultural Society at Chiswick and illustrated in Ronalds (1831) where it was also described as a Shropshire apple.

The fruit will keep until March but is at its best before Christmas as it becomes rather dry later. The tree is a slow grower and, according to Hogg, never attains a great size but bears regular crops on numerous short spurs.

Size	*Small-medium to medium (55–60 × 50mm)*		Cavity	*Regular, lined with thick, often scaly, brown russet*
Shape	*Conical or round-conical, regular or sometimes with obscure blunt ribs ending in low crowns*		Stalk	*Fairly short, usually within cavity or level with base, with rounded or flared-truncate tip*
Skin	*Ground colour greenish-yellow, becoming red with crimson streaks in the sun, dry and usually extensively covered with thin brown russet*		Flesh	*Deep-cream, firm and rather dry, with sweet, rich, aromatic flavour*
Lenticels	*Round, fairly small but raised so that the surface feels rough*		Tube	*Short, conical or funnel-shaped, with stamens median or towards basal*
Basin	*Rather broad and shallow, sometimes grooved or puckered*		Core	*Median, with broad-obovate or round cells which are axile, closed; sometimes a double core line is present*
Eye	*Usually half-open, with green, erect-convergent or connivent, abruptly narrowing sepals with reflexed tips*		Seeds	*Plump, rounded, blunt or apiculate, (7–8mm)*
			Flowers	*Pollination group 3 (11)*

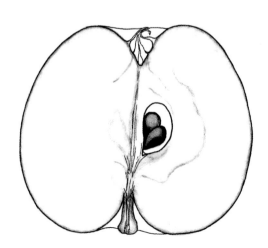
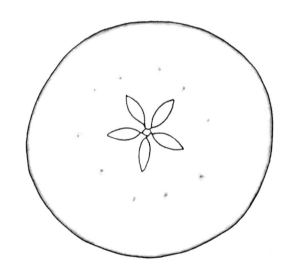

BYFORD WONDER

Late culinary

THIS handsome, vigorous, triploid variety gained an Award of Merit from the Royal Horticultural Society when it was exhibited in 1893. It was introduced in 1894 by Cranston & Co. (King's Acre Nurseries) of Hereford. The apple is named after the village of Byford on the north bank of the River Wye, 10 kilometres upstream.

The fruit should be picked in early October and is in season from November to January. When cooked the pieces retain their shape and have a delicate flavour, described in Morgan and Richards (1993) as pear-like.

Size	*Large or very large (90 × 70mm)*
Shape	*Flat-round, regular or slightly angular*
Skin	*Smooth, pale yellow with an orange flush (up to 20%), traces of pale greyish-brown russet may be present*
Lenticels	*Fairly conspicuous as irregular pale greyish dots scattered over the fruit*
Basin	*Wide, regular, sometimes lined with russet*
Eye	*Medium, partly open, sepals erect-convergent with reflexed tips*

Cavity	*Rather wide and deep, regular, lined with pale greyish-brown russet which may spread over base*
Stalk	*Stout, within cavity, usually about level with base*
Flesh	*Cream, tender, fairly juicy and sub-acid*
Tube	*Deep and funnel-shaped (7–12mm); stamens marginal or sometimes median*
Core	*Median, small, axile-closed, cells elliptical or slightly obovate*
Seeds	*Rather sparse, often shrivelled (up to 10mm)*
Flowers	*Pollination group 2 (9)*

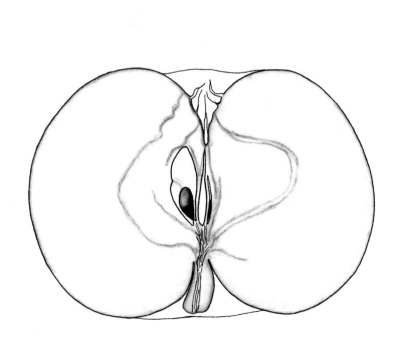
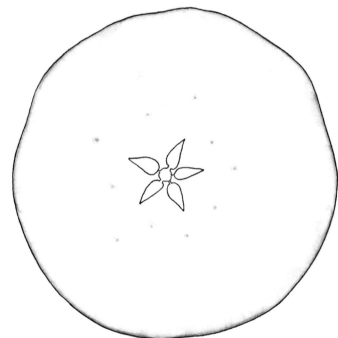

CHATLEY KERNEL

Late culinary

THIS variety became more widely known when shown by George Bunyard & Co. in the Royal Horticultural Society's Exhibition of British Grown Fruit at the Crystal Palace in 1894. At this time the variety was already listed, as CHATLEY'S KERNEL, in the catalogues of Richard Smith & Co. (Worcester) where it is described as "probably the most marvellous keeping apple in existence".

Recent research by a resident of Chatley, a hamlet in the parish of Ombersley near Worcester, has led to the discovery of several old trees of CHATLEY KERNEL in the area and it seems likely that the apple is named after this place.

It will keep in good condition until April or May and this may well be its chief virtue; Edward Bunyard (1920) concludes his account of the variety with the comment: "Hardly worthy of cultivation".

In the early years of the twentieth century nurseries, such as King's Acre (Hereford), mainly sold a bright red form of the cultivar, old trees of which are still occasionally found in farm orchards in the Welsh Marches.

Size	*Medium (68 × 54mm)*	Cavity	*Regular, lined with thin or scaly greyish-brown russet*
Shape	*Round or flat-round, generally regular but sometimes with traces of well-rounded ribs which end in low, broad crowns*	Stalk	*Usually projecting beyond base, with flared-truncate tip*
Skin	*Dry, pale green with brownish-red flush and darker stripes; sometimes a variable amount of grey-brown russet spreading from the basin or cavity onto the sides. There is also a red form in which the fruit is largely covered by a bright red flush*	Flesh	*Greenish-white, fine, firm-textured and fairly juicy, acidic*
		Tube	*Narrowly funnel-shaped and fairly deep; stamen position variable*
		Core	*Axile-closed, with broad, ovate or obovate, slightly tufted cells*
Lenticels	*Conspicuous, the largest near the base, stellate, sometimes with grey-brown areola*	Seeds	*Plentiful, large (9mm), plump, with short point, dark brown*
Basin	*Fairly regular, slightly undulating or puckered*	Flowers	*Pollination group 5 (19)*
Eye	*Usually open, sepals convergent or connivent, with reflexed tips*		

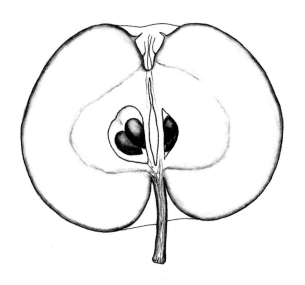
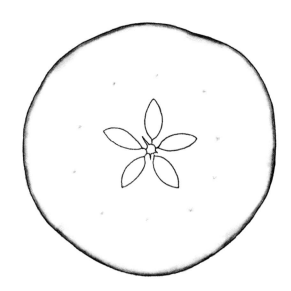

CISSY

Synonyms: *Tamplin, Tampling, Monmouthshire Beauty*

— *Mid-season dessert* —

ACCORDING to Basham (1899) this variety was raised in the 1790s by a Mr. Tampling of Malpas, near Newport, Monmouthshire. His sister Cissy continued distributing grafts after his death. Basham also records that this was one of the favourite varieties grown for market in parts of Monmouthshire at the end of the nineteenth century. When it was sent from Abergavenny for exhibition as MONMOUTHSHIRE BEAUTY at the National Apple Congress in 1883, it was listed in both dessert and culinary categories as a variety suitable for growing in Monmouthshire. However, attempts to impose the name MONMOUTHSHIRE BEAUTY at some shows evoked a hostile reaction from local people. As TAMPLIN, it received an Award of Merit from the Royal Horticultural Society in 1902.

The apples, which are borne mainly at the tips of branches, are ripe in September and in a good season the fruit has a fine aromatic flavour, but not highly rated by Edward Bunyard. In some areas the variety seems to be susceptible to apple scab.

Size	*Medium (65 × 55mm)*		Stalk	*Level with base or slightly projecting*
Shape	*Round or round-conical, regular and symmetrical*		Flesh	*Deep cream, faintly green around the core, crisp and juicy, with pleasant aromatic flavour*
Skin	*Smooth, with yellow ground colour largely obscured by crimson flush and short dark-red streaks*		Tube	*Funnel-shaped (8–9mm), with stamens median or slightly marginal*
Lenticels	*Rather indistinct, small, brown*		Core	*Median, axile-closed or occasionally axile-open, with round cells*
Basin	*Fairly shallow, often puckered or beaded*			
Eye	*Closed, with erect-convergent sepals which may have reflexed tips*		Seeds	*Plentiful, plump, acute, chestnut brown, (8–9mm)*
Cavity	*Deep, regular, lined with brown russet which may spread over the base*		Flowers	*Pollination group 3 (11)*

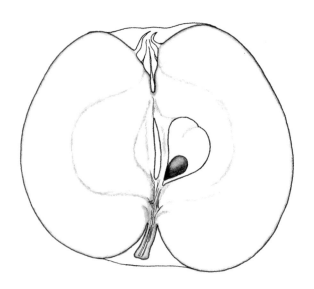

COLWALL QUOINING

— *Mid-late season dessert* —

GRAFTWOOD of COLWALL QUOINING was sent to the National Fruit Collections from Tenbury Wells in Worcestershire in 1949. It is named after a village near Great Malvern, but its early history is unknown. As Knight (1811) commented in his description of the OLD QUINING: "Many varieties of apples have been classed under the name Quining in Herefordshire… all of which are distinguished by their angular shape and by a very strong aromatic smell and flavour". The quoinings, quinings or queenings are an ancient group and discrepancies in their descriptions have often led to confusion over the identification of the various sorts. Hogg (1884) describes five varieties, none of which match COLWALL QUOINING, and only two of which appear to be extant. However, at least five sorts still grow in local orchards, so there is fertile ground for further research.

Trees of COLWALL QUOINING are vigorous growers and regularly produce heavy crops. The fruit is in season from October to January and produces a flavoursome juice.

Size	*Medium to medium-large (70 × 65mm)*		Cavity	*Usually regular, sometimes lipped, narrow, deep, often lined with brown russet*
Shape	*Conical or round-conical, with ribs extending from the base and ending in prominent, often unequal, crowns*		Stalk	*Long (to 25mm), flared truncate at tip, usually projecting beyond base*
Skin	*Smooth, waxy, ground colour yellow, largely covered by red flush and dark-red stripes*		Flesh	*White, juicy, with rich, distinctive flavour*
			Tube	*Broadly conical; stamens median or basal*
Lenticels	*Mainly small, oval or irregular, generally not conspicuous*		Core	*Large, usually open-axile, with obovate or elliptical cells*
Basin	*Rather narrow, ribbed and puckered*		Seeds	*Large (9mm), plump, acute*
Eye	*Medium-large, closed with green-based sepals connivent, with some tips spreading or reflexed*		Flowers	*Pollination group 4 (14)*

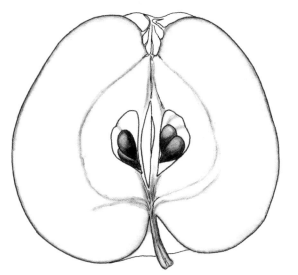

CREDENHILL PIPPIN

— *Late dessert* —

THIS variety was raised, about 1896, either by Frank Whiting, or his father Richard, at Credenhill, a village six kilometres northwest of Hereford. Frank's notebook indicates that he had eight trees of CREDENHILL PIPPIN growing in his nursery in 1901, when the variety was first displayed at the Annual Exhibition of British Grown Fruit. Taylor (1946) has a brief description of CREDENHILL PIPPIN and notes that it is "a purely local variety raised by Mr. Whiting of Hereford" and not listed in the catalogues of nursery firms.

In 2001 a tree of this variety was found in an orchard less than two kilometres from Credenhill, when the owner brought in fruit for identification at an Apple Day event at Much Marcle.

The apple is ripe in November and under good storage conditions will keep until February.

Size	*Medium-large (70 × 60mm)*	Cavity	*Regular, lined by fine olive-brown russet which may spread out over base*
Shape	*Round-conical, rarely with trace of blunt ribs*	Stalk	*Usually projecting beyond base, straight or slightly flared at tip*
Skin	*Smooth, dry, ground colour yellow, usually half-covered by a red flush and bold dark-red stripes; some pale greyish-brown russet present*	Flesh	*Creamy-yellow, firm, juicy, with pleasant but fairly plain flavour*
Lenticels	*Small, round or angular, pale grey, widespread and fairly conspicuous*	Tube	*Funnel-shaped (7–9mm); stamens median or slightly marginal*
Basin	*Regular or slightly puckered, sometimes with fine pale russet*	Core	*Usually basal, axile-closed, with broad ovate, tufted cells*
Eye	*Medium-large, open, sepals erect or erect-convergent with reflexed tips*	Seeds	*Large (9mm), plump, acute*
		Flowers	*Pollination group 3 (13–14)*

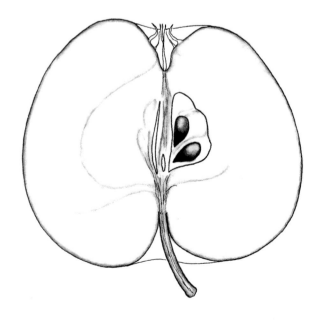
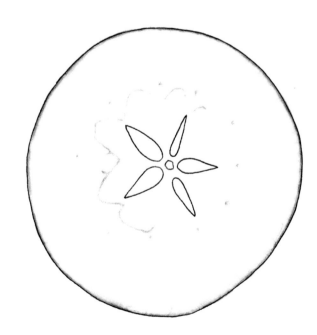

FORESTER

Late culinary

HOGG (1884) records that FORESTER "is much grown in the south of Shropshire and north of Worcestershire". Curiously the variety was not included in *The Herefordshire Pomona* (1875–1886). It was possibly a fairly recent introduction when large, fine examples from Pershore and Eardiston in Worcestershire were exhibited at the National Apple Congress at Chiswick in 1883. On that occasion FORESTER was selected by a panel of local growers as one of the culinary varieties recommended for cultivation in Worcestershire. By the turn of the century it was being grown for the market in several orchards around Hereford and specimens from John Watkins of Pomona Farm, Hereford, were exhibited at the Royal Horticultural Society in 1895.

FORESTER is a robust grower and reliable cropper. The fruit will keep in good condition until January. It cooks to a thick, yellow-green purée which has a very good flavour.

Size	*Medium-large (75 × 61mm)*	Cavity	*Regular, wide and deep, lined with greenish-grey russet spreading out over base*
Shape	*Flattened round-conical, regular or with blunt ribs which end in low rounded crowns or form a ridge around the basin*	Stalk	*Variable in length, fairly stout, truncate, within cavity or level with base*
Skin	*Dry, usually smooth, ground colour greenish-yellow with orange-brown flush and variable amounts of fine, pale golden-brown russet*	Flesh	*Creamy-yellow, tinged green under skin and around core, rather soft, sub-acid*
		Tube	*Funnel-shaped; stamens marginal or median*
Lenticels	*Not prominent, small, round or oval grey-brown dots*	Core	*Axile open or closed, with broad ovate or round cells*
Basin	*Ribbed or puckered*	Seeds	*Rather small (6–7mm), usually blunt*
Eye	*Medium size, closed, with sepals erect-convergent with tips curved back*	Flowers	*Pollination group 4 (16)*

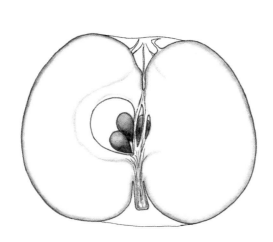
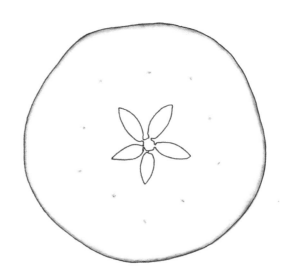

GREEN PURNELL

— *Late dessert* —

LITTLE is known about the history of this triploid variety. According to Smith (1971) it was received by the National Fruit Trials, from Worcestershire, in 1945, and was reputed to be an old variety.

The accession notes record that GREEN PURNELL was supplied by the writer and broadcaster Morton Shand, a connoisseur of apples, cider and wine and an enthusiatic collector of rare old varieties.

The fruit is ripe in November and will keep until the end of January.

Size	*Medium-large (70 × 56mm)*	Cavity	*Regular, lined with rather scaly pale brown russet which may spread over base*
Shape	*Round or round-conical, fairly regular*	Stalk	*Medium thickness, level with base or projecting, straight or flared*
Skin	*Pale greenish-yellow, sometimes with orange-red flush and pale red streaks, traces of thin pale brown russet*	Flesh	*Cream, firm, fine-textured, sweet and fairly juicy*
Lenticels	*Irregular, grey, more noticeable on yellow background; on red parts lenticels are surrounded by yellow areola*	Tube	*Conical, stamens median*
		Core	*Median or basal, axile, open or closed, cells broadly obovate or round*
Basin	*Regular or slightly puckered*	Seeds	*Sparse, medium to small (7mm)*
Eye	*Medium-small, half open, with short erect-convergent green sepals*	Flowers	*Pollination group 3 (12)*

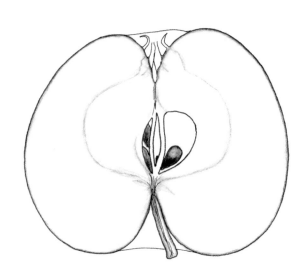
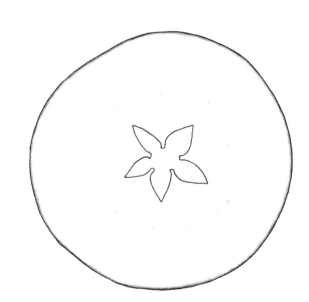

HUNT'S DUKE OF GLOUCESTER

Late dessert

THIS delicious variety was raised by Dr. Fry of Gloucester from a pip of NONPAREIL and named after Thomas Hunt of Stratford-on-Avon who sent specimens to the Horticultural Society of London in 1820. HUNT'S DUKE OF GLOUCESTER was grown in the gardens of the Royal Horticultural Society at Chiswick until the late nineteenth century and is described in some detail in Lindley (1831) and Hogg (1851 and later editions). Study of these early accounts indicates that sometime during the twentieth century the names of HUNT'S DUKE OF GLOUCESTER and PUCKRUPP PIPPIN were transposed, and in recent years the identity of these varieties has become confused.

HUNT'S DUKE OF GLOUCESTER forms a slender, upright tree. The fruit should be picked in October and is in season from November until February or March. It has an excellent flavour, contrasting sweetness and acidity, similar to that of NONPAREIL.

Size	*Small-medium (58 × 50mm)*
Shape	*Round-conical to oblong-conical or oblong, regular or obscurely ribbed towards apex and occasionally with low crowns*
Skin	*Ground colour green on the shaded side, with flush of brownish-red on the sunny side (15%), but most of surface covered by fine brown russet (>80%)*
Lenticels	*Round, not prominent, mainly hidden under russet, pale brown on red background, brown on green*
Basin	*Shallow, even or slightly ribbed or puckered*
Eye	*Medium, partly or fully open, with erect or erect-convergent sepals, which may have reflexed tips*
Cavity	*Regular or sometimes lipped, narrowing abruptly, lined with fine olive-brown russet*
Stalk	*Slender, usually projecting beyond base, flared-truncate at tip*
Flesh	*White tinged with green, fine, tender, juicy, with a very good flavour*
Tube	*Funnel-shaped, with narrow stem (7mm); stamens marginal or sometimes median*
Core	*Basal, axile-closed, cells broadly obovate or round, tufted*
Seeds	*Long (9–10mm), straight-sided, acuminate*
Flowers	*Pollination group 3 (10)*

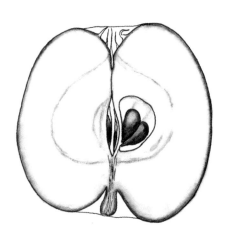

KING COFFEE

APPLES of this variety from East Malling were exhibited at the Fruit Conference of the Royal Horticultural Society held at the Crystal Palace in 1934. In 1937, grafts of KING COFFEE were supplied to the National Fruit Trials by E. W. Hobbies, a Horticultural Instructor for Worcestershire County Council, who noted that the variety had been grown in Worcestershire for many years.

Fruit is ripe in November and December, but the coffee flavour is sometimes faint and difficult to detect.

Size	*Medium-large to large (73 × 60mm)*		Cavity	*Wide, regular, lined with greenish-brown russet which may streak over base*
Shape	*Flat-round to flat-conical, regular*		Stalk	*Fairly stout, within cavity or level with base*
Skin	*Smooth, dry, ground colour greenish-yellow, with dark maroon flush (up to 90%) and dark-red streaks, thin brown russet in basin*		Flesh	*Greenish-white, juicy, rather sweet, sometimes slightly bittersweet; in the transverse section the carpel threads and Truelle line are often green*
Lenticels	*Small and crowded at apex, larger, stellate and less dense at base, fairly conspicuous on dark background*		Tube	*Conical, stamens median*
Basin	*Wide, shallow, regular or slightly puckered, sometimes lined by concentric brown russet*		Core	*Median, axile-closed, cells obovate*
			Seeds	*Rather narrow and straight-sided (8–9mm)*
Eye	*Medium, usually partly open, sepals small, erect or erect-convergent with recurved tips*		Flowers	*Pollination group 4 (17)*

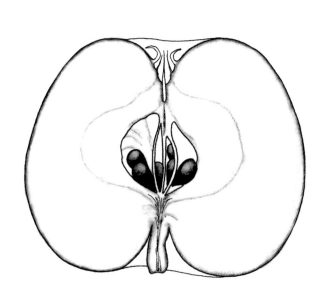

KING'S ACRE BOUNTIFUL

Mid-season culinary

THE cultivar was raised from a seedling of unknown parentage and introduced by King's Acre Nurseries, Hereford, in 1904. When exhibited for the first time, at the British Hardy-Grown Fruit Show at the Horticultural Hall, London, it received an Award of Merit from the Royal Horticultural Society.

Having been enthusiastically promoted by King's Acre Nurseries, it is still to be found in many gardens and orchards in Herefordshire and surrounding counties. It is a healthy, robust variety which grows into a compact tree, flowering late and a regular cropper.

The apples are in season from September to November and are delicious as a sharp purée or roasted to make succulent baked apples.

Size	*Large or very large (85 × 66mm)*
Shape	*Round or flat-round, with obscure ribs ending in low crowns around the basin*
Skin	*Smooth and waxy, with extensive white bloom when unripe, ground colour green becoming cream or pale yellow, sometimes a pink flush (up to 15%)*
Lenticels	*Small, round, pale grey or dark green, sometimes surrounded by pale areola*
Basin	*Fairly regular, often ribbed, sometimes puckered or beaded*
Eye	*Medium, closed, sometimes appearing pinched, with small erect-convergent or connivent sepals with reflexed tips*

Cavity	*Wide, regular or ribbed, sometimes with fine grey-brown russet which may spread to base*
Stalk	*Short, stout and sometimes fleshy, usually within cavity, sometimes projecting and with a rounded tip*
Flesh	*White with green tinge, juicy, acidic*
Tube	*Broadly conical (7mm); stamens median or slightly marginal*
Core	*Median, axile, closed or open, cells round or broadly obovate*
Seeds	*Plump, acute, mid-brown (7–8mm)*
Flowers	*Pollination group 6 (23)*

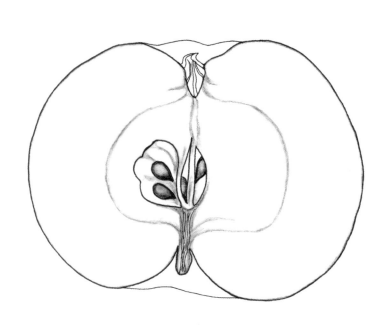
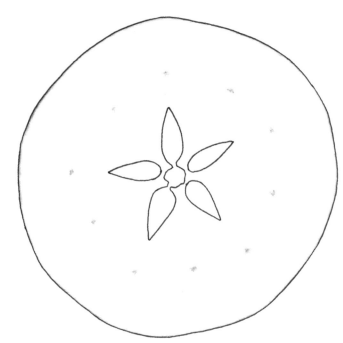

LANDORE

Synonym: *Monmouth Green*

— *Late dessert and culinary* —

THIS variety has been grown in Herefordshire and the neighbouring Welsh counties since the middle of the nineteenth century or earlier. Mature trees can still be found in farm orchards around the Black Mountains and along the middle reaches of the Wye valley. The Reverend Francis Kilvert, curate of Clyro, near Hay-on-Wye, mentions in an entry in his diary on 26th February 1872 that during a visit to the local miller he was given "...three Landore apples, an old fashioned keeping apple, very good". The variety is still highly regarded by many country people, because trees produce good crops under poor conditions for apple cultivation. Young trees grow vigorously but are slow to start bearing fruit.

LANDORE appears to be one of the Underleaf group of apples. In a list of "Local Varieties of Cider Apples" in the *Herefordshire Pomona*, there is an entry for UNDERLEAF (Herefordshire) which has features in common with LANDORE, but the description is too brief to allow certain identification.

The fruit is ripe from the end of October and will keep until February. It cooks to a greenish-yellow purée, but does not break down completely.

Size	*Medium-large (70 × 60mm)*	Cavity	*Regular or ribbed, lined with fine grey russet which may spread over base*
Shape	*Round or oblong, well rounded ribs, more marked near apex where they end in irregular low crowns*	Stalk	*Stout, long, usually projecting beyond base, with flared truncate tip*
Skin	*Smooth, waxy, green becoming yellow when ripe, sometimes with a golden-brown flush on the sunny side*	Flesh	*White with green tinge, fairly dense, sub-acid, with a rather plain taste*
Lenticels	*Abundant and conspicuous, round, dark grey-brown*	Tube	*Broadly conical, stamens median*
		Core	*Basal or median, axile-closed but often becoming open later, obovate cells, prominent Truelle line*
Basin	*Slightly ribbed or puckered*	Seeds	*Large (10–12mm), plump, acute or acuminate, rather straight sided*
Eye	*Medium-large, closed, with large connivent sepals with recurved tips*	Flowers	*Pollination group 4 (14)*

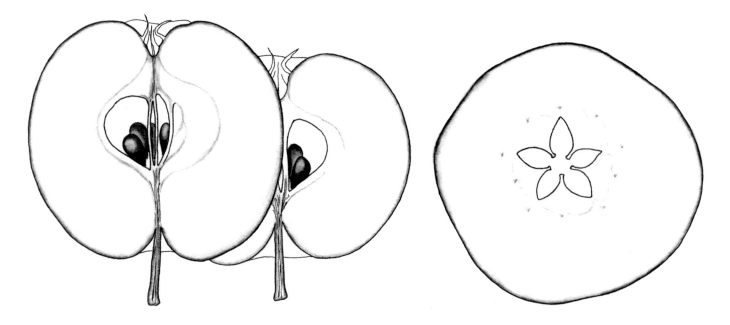

MARGED NICOLAS

Synonym: *Morgan Nicolas*

— Late dessert and culinary —

AS is the case with most of the old Welsh varieties, little is known about the history of this apple. Trees which are more than seventy years old are growing in farm orchards in Dinefwr, in the east of Dyfed. Young trees are upright growing with a narrow crown but old trees develop a characteristic fountain-like appearance with arching branches.

Fruit is ripe in November and will keep until February. It is a general purpose fruit which can also be used for making cider.

Size	*Medium-large (70 × 54mm)*	Eye	*Small to medium, open or partly open, small sepals erect with recurved tips*
Shape	*Flat-round or flat-conical, often with obscure ribs and low crowns*	Cavity	*Fairly regular, lined with grey or grey-green russet which may spread over base*
Skin	*Dry, slightly rough, ground colour yellow with golden flush on the sunny side. Concentric flecks of brownish-grey russet around the eye, becoming sparser lower down the cheeks*	Stalk	*Short, broad and often fleshy, within cavity*
		Flesh	*Cream, firm, rather dry, sweet*
		Tube	*Conical (7–9mm); stamens basal*
		Core	*Variable in position, small, usually axile-closed, with round, tufted cells*
Lenticels	*Greyish-brown, irregular or stellate, difficult to distinguish from russet specks*	Seeds	*Plentiful, broad and rather blunt (7–8mm), mid-brown*
Basin	*Ribbed, puckered and sometimes beaded, with russet in grooves, green colour remaining late at base of sepals*	Flowers	*Pollination group 4 (15)*

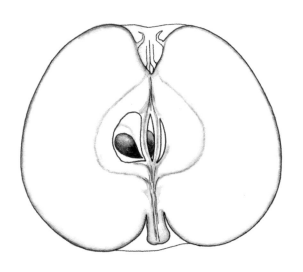

NEW GERMAN

— *Late culinary* —

THE only historical description discovered is that of Hogg (1884), which shows slight differences from the NEW GERMAN in the National Fruit Collections at Brogdale, on which our account is based. Hogg concludes his account by recording that NEW GERMAN is "a good useful Herefordshire apple up till Christmas".

Rather surprisingly, the variety was not included in *The Herefordshire Pomona* which was edited by Hogg. A large, late apple named GERMAN was illustrated in a preliminary painting intended for the *Pomona*, and that variety was exhibited from Hereford in the 1883 National Apple Congress at Chiswick, so there appears to have been some debate about the apple at that time.

As might be expected from a triploid variety, NEW GERMAN grows vigorously to form a spreading tree. The large, colourful fruit are borne freely and, though rather sharp early in the season, become sweeter in late autumn.

Size	*Large or very large (84 × 65mm)*		Cavity	*Wide, regular or ridged, lined with brown or greenish-brown russet which is sometimes scaly and often streaks out over base*
Shape	*Flat-round to round, bluntly-angular with ribs extended to form broad, uneven crowns*		Stalk	*Generally stout, variable in length but often level with base or protruding*
Skin	*Smooth, waxy becoming greasy, ground colour pale yellow, largely obscured by red flush and streaks and splashes of dark red or maroon*		Flesh	*White tinged green, tender, juicy, acidic at first but becoming subacid or sweet*
Lenticels	*Small, oval or round, not conspicuous*		Tube	*Deep, broad cone with stamens median or marginal*
Basin	*Fairly deep, ridged and puckered and sometimes beaded*		Core	*Large, axile-open or abaxile, cells ovate*
			Seeds	*Medium size, acute (7mm)*
Eye	*Medium to large, closed, with erect-convergent sepals with recurved tips*		Flowers	*Pollination group 3 (11)*

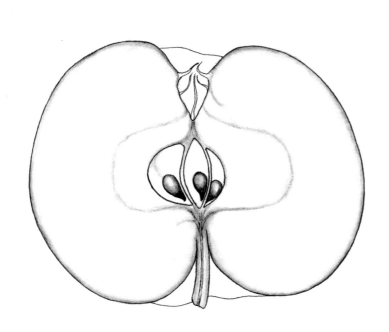

NEWLAND SACK

—— *Late culinary or dessert* ——

MOST of our information about the history of NEWLAND SACK comes from *The Herefordshire Pomona* where it is recorded that the variety arose, about 1800, from a pip in a heap of pomace (pulp discarded from a cider press) at Newland Court near Great Malvern. The variety was prized for its keeping quality: "An excellent culinary apple, in season throughout the winter, and keeps well until May, without any tendency to decay, even when bruised". After Christmas the smaller apples were sold as dessert fruit.

It was exhibited at the Apple and Pear Conference of the Royal Horticultural Society in 1888, by William Crump, Head Gardener at nearby Madresfield Court, the estate which owned Newland Court.

NEWLAND SACK was said to be very hardy and to produce heavy crops. The farmer at Newland Court in the 1880s was quoted as saying "it is the best family apple known" and expressed the wish that all his orchards were of NEWLAND SACKS and BLENHEIM PIPPINS. Despite all its good qualities, in recent years NEWLAND SACK has almost disappeared from the area. In 2001 a single, venerable but decrepit tree was found to have survived at Newland Court.

Size	*Medium-large (70 × 62mm)*	Cavity	*Often irregular, lined with dark greyish-brown russet which may spread over base*
Shape	*Round-conical or conical, asymmetrical, broad unequal ribs ending in prominent crowns*	Stalk	*Level with base or protruding, usually stout, with flared-truncate tip*
Skin	*Smooth, except where russeted, ground colour greenish-yellow, sometimes with orange or vermilion flush (up to 25%); patches of rough greyish brown russet over base sometimes spreading up the sides*	Flesh	*Cream or greenish-white, tender, sub-acid, pleasant slightly aromatic flavour*
		Tube	*Usually funnel-shaped; marginal stamens*
Lenticels	*Small or medium, round or irregular, dark grey, conspicuous on yellow ground*	Core	*Basal or median, axile-closed, may become axile-open later, with obovate or elliptical, tufted cells*
Basin	*Narrow, deep, ribbed and often puckered*	Seeds	*Rather straight-sided, acute or apiculate (9mm)*
Eye	*Medium to large, closed, long narrow connivent sepals with tips recurved*	Flowers	*Pollination group 3 (10); very attractive pink blossom*

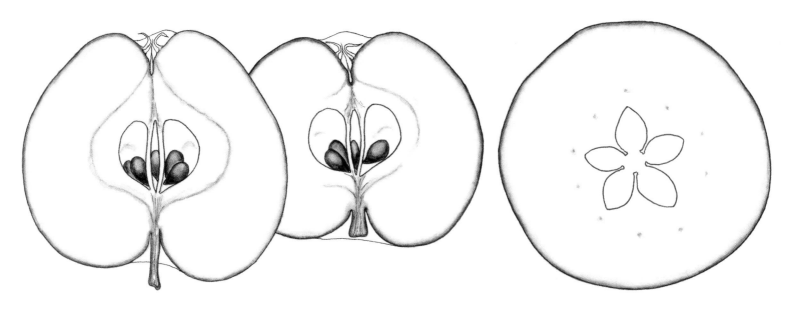

ONIBURY PIPPIN

—— Mid-season dessert ——

NAMED after the village of Onibury near Ludlow, the cultivar is reputed to have been raised nearby in one of Thomas Andrew Knight's nurseries in the early part of the nineteenth century. Tillington Nurseries showed the variety at the Apple and Pear Exhibition at Hereford, organised by the Woolhope Club in 1883 and a report described ONIBURY PIPPIN as "a perfect model for a dessert apple from its handsome neat looks, golden colour and lasting qualities". The apple was figured in a preliminary watercolour for *The Herefordshire Pomona* but did not appear in the published work.

The variety was on display at the Royal Horticultural Society's Fruit Conference at the Crystal Palace in 1934, but disappeared from the horticultural scene until rediscovered by a Shropshire tree warden in 1996.

The juicy, refreshing fruit is ripe in October and November.

Size	*Medium (63 × 58mm)*
Shape	*Oblong, flattened at both ends, regular or with obscure ribs ending in low crowns*
Skin	*Dry and smooth, ground colour yellow, sometimes with a dark golden flush on the sunny side (up to 30% in extent). Patches of fine greyish-brown russet in the basin and on the sides. A hairline may be present*
Lenticels	*Conspicuous, round, medium sized grey-brown dots scattered over fruit*
Basin	*Broad, shallow, saucer-shaped, often slightly puckered or beaded*
Eye	*Medium to large, closed, with long, narrow, erect-convergent or connivent sepals with reflexed tips*

Cavity	*Deep and regular or sometimes lipped, lined with fine grey-brown russet*
Stalk	*Stout, with a flared-truncate tip; variable in length, but usually projecting beyond base*
Flesh	*Creamy-white, soft in texture, like that of BLENHEIM ORANGE but juicier*
Tube	*A short cone (6–7mm) with marginal or median stamens*
Core	*Axile, closed, with obovate or round tufted cells*
Seeds	*Mid-brown, long (9–10mm), narrow and straight-sided, blunt or acuminate*
Flowers	*Pollination group 4 (15)*

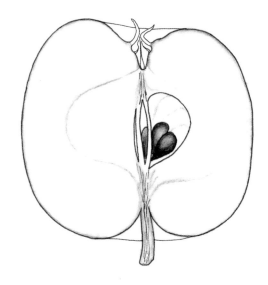
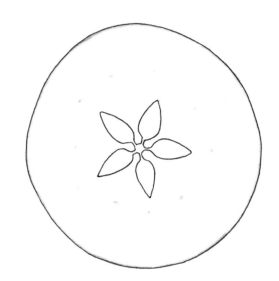

PIG'S NOSE PIPPIN

— Late dessert —

THIS apple is described in Hogg (1884) as "a pretty little dessert apple, grown about Hereford, which keeps in use till Christmas". The variety is not described in *The Herefordshire Pomona*, nor is it mentioned by other Victorian authors. Hogg underestimates its keeping quality, as it often remains in good condition until the end of February.

It grows rather slowly into a small tree with slender branches bearing fruit mainly at their tips.

Size	*Small to medium (55 × 50mm)*	Cavity	*Regular, lined with dense greyish-brown russet which often spreads over base*
Shape	*Conical, regular, flat at base and apex*	Stalk	*Medium thickness, level with base or projecting, with rounded or flared tip*
Skin	*Smooth, dry, ground colour pale yellow with red flush (up to 80%) and short narrow scarlet streaks, fine pale greyish-brown russet in basin and cavity, sometimes patches of russet on the cheeks*	Flesh	*Cream, tinged green, with green core-line, firm, fine-textured, juicy, with a pleasant sweet and faintly aromatic flavour*
Lenticels	*Small, round or oval, greyish-brown, fairly conspicuous on yellow background*	Tube	*Short, funnel-shaped (5mm); stamens median*
Basin	*Broad, shallow, regular or slightly puckered*	Core	*Basal, axile-closed, with obovate, tufted cells*
		Seeds	*Long (10mm), rather narrow and straight-sided*
Eye	*Medium-large, open, sepals erect with recurved tips*	Flowers	*Pollination group 4 (14)*

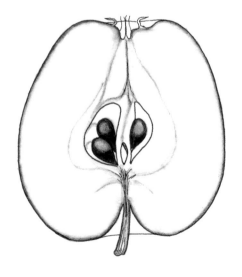
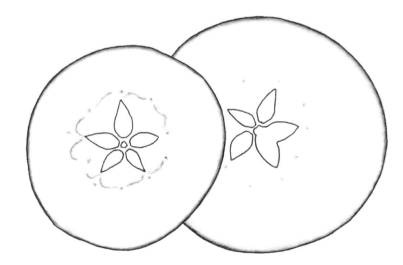

PIG YR WŶDD

— Mid-season culinary —

MATURE trees of PIG YR WŶDD are growing in several farm orchards in the Dinefwr region of Dyfed. The trees are vigorous and produce heavy crops. Branches produce burrs at the base which, under damp conditions, may develop roots, allowing them to be detached and grown into separate trees. Several Welsh varieties that show this potential for vegetative propagation are called 'pitchers' in South Wales.

The fruit is in season from September until Christmas. It cooks to a thick purée, retaining plenty of acidity, even at the end of the year.

PIG YR WŶDD may be translated as 'goose's beak', the name being inspired by the angles and curves on the sides of the fruit.

Size	*Medium-large (70 × 65mm)*	Cavity	*Shallow, often strongly lipped so that stalk is deflected sideways*
Shape	*Round-conical or oblong-conical, angular, with unequal ribs ending in prominent crowns*	Stalk	*Often fleshy, projecting obliquely or fused*
Skin	*Smooth, dry, ground colour yellow-green, with orange flush and short scarlet streaks (up to 60%). About 25% show a hair-line running part or all the way from basin to cavity*	Flesh	*Greenish-white, firm, fairly juicy, sharply acid*
		Tube	*Conical; marginal stamens*
Lenticels	*Fairly conspicuous, small, round, dark grey or green, sometimes surrounded by pale areola*	Core	*Distant, fairly small, usually axile-open becoming abaxile, cells narrow, elliptical*
Basin	*Rather narrow, ribbed, puckered or beaded, often with fine grey-brown russet*	Seeds	*Fairly long (9–10mm), acute or acuminate, sometimes with curved tips*
Eye	*Closed, sepals long and narrow, erect-convergent with recurved or spreading tips*	Flowers	*Pollination group 2 (9)*

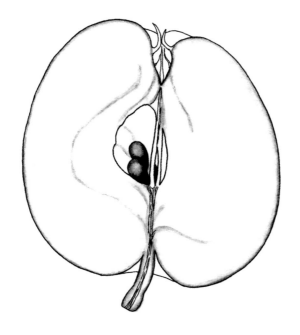

POMEROY OF HEREFORDSHIRE

Synonyms: *Pineapple Russet of Devon; Pomeroy; Sussex Peach*

―――――― *Mid-season dessert* ――――――

POMEROY, a corruption of POMME DU ROI (King's Apple), is an ancient name which occurs in the lists of seventeenth century authors such as Ray and Langford. There has been much confusion about the identity of apples bearing this name. Hogg (1884) refers to three different POMEROYS associated with various regions. The variety represented here is called POMEROY in *The Herefordshire Pomona*, and POMEROY OF HEREFORDSHIRE in Hogg (1884). This variety does not appear in the earlier editions of *The Fruit Manual*, compiled before Hogg's detailed study of Herefordshire apples.

According to Smith (1971) POMEROY OF HEREFORDSHIRE was in the National Fruit Trials as SUSSEX PEACH and morphologically indistinguishable from PINEAPPLE RUSSET OF DEVON.

POMEROY OF HEREFORDSHIRE grows rapidly into a large spreading tree, which when young has a smooth golden-brown bark. The fruit is ripe in late September and October and has a distinctive and delicious flavour. In some parts of Herefordshire the variety is known as SUGAR APPLE.

Size	*Medium to medium-large (70 × 60mm)*		Cavity	*Wide, fairly deep, lined with scaly brown russet which often spreads over base*
Shape	*Round or round-conical, often with blunt ribs ending in low, unequal crowns*		Stalk	*Usually within cavity or level with base, flared-truncate or rounded at tip*
Skin	*Dry, rough, ground colour pale glaucous green becoming pale yellow, with a pinkish-red blush (up to 50%), some red streaks, a large patch of cinnamon russet and traces of netted russet; a hairline is present in a small proportion*		Flesh	*Yellow, soft, sometimes rather dry, with a distinctive pineapple flavour*
			Tube	*Conical or slightly funnel-shaped (7–9mm); stamens median, sometimes marginal*
			Core	*Median or basal, axile-closed, later abaxile, cells elliptical-round, tufted; core line often double*
Lenticels	*Small and round at apex, larger and irregular towards base*			
Basin	*Ribbed or puckered, often beaded*		Seeds	*Rather straight-sided, acute or blunt (8–9mm)*
Eye	*Medium, closed, sepals erect-convergent, with narrow tips recurved*		Flowers	*Pollination group 3 (12)*

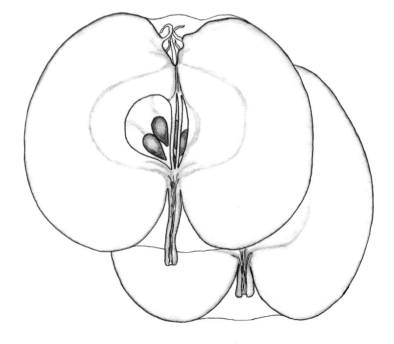
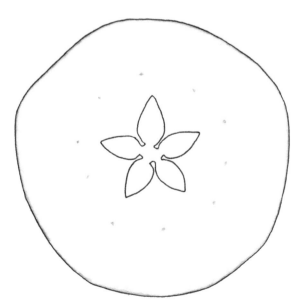

PUCKRUPP PIPPIN

— Late dessert —

THIS attractive dessert apple appears to have been first described by Scott (1873) but there is no indication of its history or provenance. His account is brief but records key features of the variety. PUCKRUPP PIPPIN was also listed in the 1880-1 catalogue of Richard Smith & Co. of Worcester and it seems likely that the variety originated in the hamlet of Puckrup about 14 kilometres south of Worcester. Both nurserymen reported that trees of PUCKRUPP PIPPIN bore heavy crops and the fruit had an excellent flavour.

Although the varieties differ in many ways, in recent times PUCKRUPP PIPPIN has been confused with HUNT'S DUKE OF GLOUCESTER.

Young trees tend to overcrop and thinning is necessary to ensure larger fruit and avoid a tendency to biennial bearing. Fruit is in season from November until January.

Size	*Medium or small-medium (60 × 50mm)*	Cavity	*Regular, lined with cinnamon-brown russet; green colour remains longest in cavity and basin*
Shape	*Round-conical to round, fairly regular, sometimes with a trace of blunt ribs*	Stalk	*Short, usually within cavity, occasionally projecting beyond base, rounded or flared at tip*
Skin	*Dry, rough, ground colour yellow, almost covered with cinnamon-brown russet but the yellow ground colour showing through in patches, especially at the apex*	Flesh	*Cream, firm, juicy, with an excellent aromatic flavour*
		Tube	*Conical or slightly funnel-shaped (6–7mm); stamens marginal*
Lenticels	*Raised round or oval lenticels apparent near base and sometimes evident in yellow-green patches elsewhere on fruit*	Core	*Median, axile-closed, with broadly obovate or almost round tufted cells*
Basin	*Regular or slightly puckered, often remaining green at base of sepals*	Seeds	*Dark-brown, plump, sometimes rather blunt (6–8mm)*
Eye	*Small-medium, open or closed, long narrow connivent sepals with reflexed tips*	Flowers	*Pollination group 2 (8)*

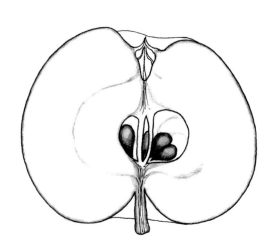

SAM'S CRAB

Synonym: *Longville's Kernel*

— *Early dessert and cider* —

THIS popular Herefordshire apple was cultivated in the gardens of the Royal Horticultural Society at Chiswick in the early nineteenth century and there is a description of it, accompanied by an excellent coloured illustration, in the *Pomological Magazine* (1828). Until the publication of *The Herefordshire Pomona* (1885) most authors referred to it as LONGVILLE'S KERNEL, adding SAM'S CRAB as a synonym.

Local people preferred the name SAM'S CRAB. On 21st September 1870, Reverend Francis Kilvert noted in his diary that when he visited John Morgan, an old soldier, veteran of the Peninsular Wars, he was given "some Sam's Crabs and Quinins".

In *The Herefordshire Pomona* it is recorded that SAM'S CRAB is "well known in Herefordshire, widely distributed and highly esteemed as a very early dessert fruit …It is a prime favourite with all Herefordshire school children (no mean judges of a good Apple), and it is equally attractive to birds and insects, who revel in its sweetness".

The apple remained popular with Herefordshire schoolchildren during the Second World War, and old trees can still be found in orchards and cottage gardens.

Trees crop heavily even when young; fruit is ripe from late August, but loses its flavour if stored.

Size	*Small-medium to medium (60 × 52mm)*	Cavity	*Fairly regular, occasionally lipped, lined with fine pale greyish-brown russet*
Shape	*Round-conical, sometimes oblong-conical, with obscure ribs ending in unequal crowns or forming a ridge around the basin*	Stalk	*Usually about level with base and rounded at tip or fleshy and within cavity*
Skin	*Smooth and waxy, aromatic, ground colour greenish-yellow, with orange stippled flush and short scarlet streaks (over 75%), sometimes some traces of light russet*	Flesh	*Cream, sometimes pink at apex, tender, very juicy, sweet with 'piquant' flavour*
		Tube	*Short, funnel-shaped (5–7mm), stamens median or slightly marginal*
Lenticels	*Small, round, dark-brown, inconspicuous except on yellow areas*	Core	*Median, usually axile-closed, with round or broadly obovate cells*
Basin	*Deep, ribbed or beaded*	Seeds	*Plump, blunt or acute (6–7mm)*
Eye	*Open, sepals small, erect with reflexed tips*	Flowers	*Pollination group 4 (14)*

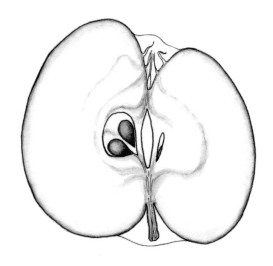 

SANDLIN DUCHESS

Late dessert and culinary

THIS handsome and colourful dual-purpose variety was raised by H. Gabb at Sandlin, Malvern, about 1880. In 1914, fruit was sent to the Royal Horticultural Society by William Crump, Head Gardener at Madresfield Court, two kilometres east of Great Malvern, and the variety received an Award of Merit.

SANDLIN DUCHESS is a triploid variety and the vigorous trees produce regular healthy crops. The fruit should be picked in mid-October and will keep in good condition until February.

As a dessert apple it has a pleasant, rather plain taste; when stewed it breaks down quickly to a flavoursome yellow purée.

Size	*Large or very large (88 × 74mm)*
Shape	*Flat-round or round-conical, obscurely ribbed, flat at base and apex*
Skin	*Smooth, matt, ground colour green becoming yellow, crimson stippled flush and short bright red streaks (50–80%), fine greyish-brown russet in basin and sometimes traces on cheeks*
Lenticels	*Small, round, dark-grey, generally not conspicuous*
Basin	*Wide, moderately deep, slightly ribbed or puckered*
Eye	*Medium, open or closed, sepals erect or erect-convergent with recurved tips*

Cavity	*Regular, wide and deep, occasionally lipped, lined with greyish-brown russet which spreads over base and sides*
Stalk	*Short, stout, straight or slightly flared, within cavity or level with base*
Flesh	*Cream tinged green, firm, fairly juicy, sub-acid*
Tube	*Slightly funnel-shaped (7–10mm), with median to basal stamens*
Core	*Basal or median, usually axile-closed, elliptical or round or broadly obovate, tufted cells*
Seeds	*Long (11mm), narrow, rather straight-sided, chestnut-brown, sometimes shrivelled*
Flowers	*Pollination group 3 (11)*

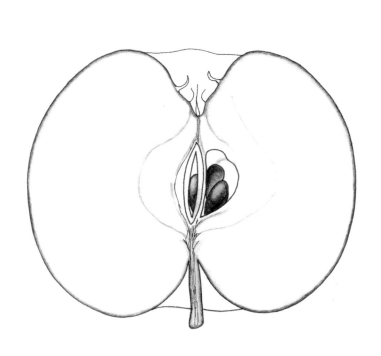

SEVERN BANK

Early to mid-season culinary

THERE are at least two other similar culinary apples known in the West Midlands as SEVERN BANK, and one of these is also used to make a bittersweet cider. The variety described here is growing in several farm orchards in Herefordshire and Gloucestershire and is also cultivated in the National Fruit Collections at Brogdale.

It matches the SEVERN BANK of Hogg (1884), who records that "it is grown in large quantities in the Valley of the Severn for the supply of the markets in the manufacturing districts, and being thick-skinned, it travels well without bruising". SEVERN BANK was not included in *The Herefordshire Pomona* but was depicted in preparatory illustrations, together with another similar variety, so there was confusion over its identity in Victorian times.

It is a triploid variety and grows strongly to produce a sturdy, well branched tree with considerable disease resistance. The fruit is in season from late August until October and cooks to a tangy purée.

Size	*Large or medium-large (75 × 60mm)*		Cavity	*Regular or slightly ribbed, often lipped (40%), lined with fine greyish-brown russet which often spreads out over base*
Shape	*Round-conical, often somewhat flattened, regular or with obscure blunt ribs ending in low crowns*		Stalk	*Broad, fleshy, within cavity or level with base, often deflected sideways*
Skin	*Smooth, slightly waxy, pale greenish-yellow with orange flush and short red streaks (up to 50%)*		Flesh	*White with green tinge, soft, coarse textured, sharp but not strongly acidic*
Lenticels	*Small, round or oval, plentiful but inconspicuous*		Tube	*Conical, with curved sides(10–14mm); stamens basal*
Basin	*Rather narrow, usually ribbed or puckered, sometimes beaded*		Core	*Median, axile-open becoming abaxile as fruit ripens, cells broadly obovate or round*
Eye	*Closed or partly open, sepals often rather pinched, erect-convergent with tips recurved*		Seeds	*Broad, acute, light to mid-brown, (8–9mm)*
			Flowers	*Pollination group 2 (8)*

STOKE EDITH PIPPIN

— Late dessert —

THIS variety was raised about 1870, probably by William Ward, Head Gardener at Stoke Edith Park, an estate some 11 kilometres east of Hereford. His employer, Lady Emily Foley, had an extensive fruit collection which supplied the Woolhope Club with specimens to illustrate *The Herefordshire Pomona*. Blossom of STOKE EDITH PIPPIN is shown in a watercolour, dated 1877, but the variety was not included in the published work.

The first record seems to be in Scott (1873), where he stated that Stock-Edith Pippin (*sic*) has not yet fruited in his nurseries at Merriott. A description of the apple is given in Hogg (1875).

John Watkins of Pomona Farm, Withington, Hereford, sent fruit of STOKE EDITH PIPPIN to the Royal Horticultural Society in 1891 and 1895. On the first occasion it was part of a collection of fifty varieties which was recommended for a Silver Banksian Medal. In 1895 his collection, which also featured FORESTER, SCARLET or CRIMSON COSTARD and WINTER QUEENING, elicited the comment that these were "varieties of fine appearance and considerable merit grown in that district, but almost unknown elsewhere".

The apple keeps well and is in season from November until February.

Size	*Medium (64 × 57mm)*	Cavity	*Fairly regular, lined with grey-brown russet which may spread on to base*
Shape	*Round-conical to conical, traces of rounded ribs ending in low, uneven crowns*	Stalk	*Variable in length and diameter, often projecting, flared-truncate at tip*
Skin	*Smooth, slightly waxy, ground colour yellow, sometimes with an orange flush (up to 30%), with a tracery of pale grey russet over cheeks*	Flesh	*Cream, firm, fine-textured, fairly juicy, fragrant and quite sweet*
Lenticels	*Small, round, grey-brown, scattered over fruit, rather conspicuous on yellow background*	Tube	*Narrow cone with curved sides or flask-shaped funnel (7–10mm); stamens marginal*
Basin	*Slightly ribbed or puckered, sometimes beaded, lined with greyish russet*	Core	*Basal, usually axile-open, cells broadly obovate or round*
Eye	*Closed or sometimes partly open, sepals long and narrow, erect-convergent with spreading or recurved tips*	Seeds	*Broad, acute or blunt, dark-brown (9–10mm)*
		Flowers	*Pollination group 3 (12)*

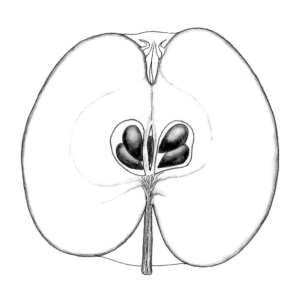

SWEENEY NONPAREIL

— *Late culinary* —

THOMAS NETHERTON PARKER of Sweeney Hall near Oswestry raised this variety in 1807. Twenty large apples from the original tree, sent to the London Horticultural Society in 1820, weighed 7lbs 13ozs. Generally the fruit collected in recent years has been smaller, but that may be because the trees are so prolific. Although described by Lindley (1831) as a dessert apple, it is too acidic for most palates until well into the spring. Hogg (1851) is closer to the mark when he writes "an excellent culinary apple admirably adapted for sauce; but too acidic for the dessert". Hogg's description of the fruit would be difficult to surpass: "Skin, of a lively green colour, which is glossy and shining, but almost entirely covered with patches and reticulations of thick greyish-brown russet, which in some parts is rough and cracked; sometimes tinged with brown where exposed to the sun".

The variety was exhibited by the Royal Horticultural Society at the National Apple Congress in 1883. Early accounts agree that SWEENEY NONPAREIL is a vigorous grower and a great bearer. Trees are upright and crop freely; fruit should be picked in mid-October and is in season from December until May. It stews to a sharp, stiff, pale-yellow purée which is ideal for apple sauce. In recent years SWEENEY NONPAREIL has been confused with BRINGEWOOD PIPPIN, though the two differ in many characters.

Size	*Medium to medium-large (72 × 56mm)*	Cavity	*Regular, with variable amount of russet*
Shape	*Round-conical, widest just above the base and tapering to eye, usually regular and symmetrical, occasionally with indistinct ribs*	Stalk	*Level with base or projecting, rather slender, with flared-truncate tip*
		Flesh	*Greenish-white, with green coreline and vascular strands, crisp, fine-textured, distinctly acidic*
Skin	*Rough, dry, ground colour bright green, extensive reticulate grey-brown russet, densest at crown and thinner below, occasionally a brown flush on the sunny side*	Tube	*Deep, narrow, conical (7–11mm); stamens marginal*
		Core	*Basal, usually axile-closed but sometimes axile-open or abaxile, cells broadly obovate*
Lenticels	*Small or medium russet dots scattered over fruit*	Seeds	*Plump, rather straight-sided, acute, mid-brown (8–9mm)*
Basin	*Narrow, regular or puckered, lined with concentric scaly brown russet*		
Eye	*Small, closed, very small connivent green sepals*	Flowers	*Pollination group 5 (19)*

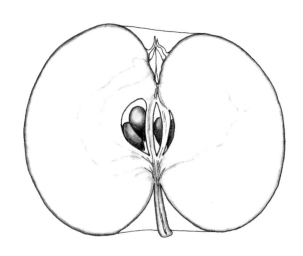
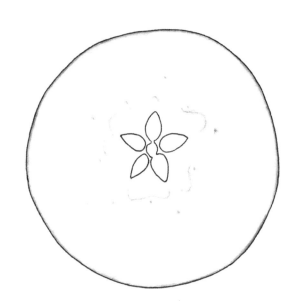

TEN COMMANDMENTS

— *Mid-season dessert and cider* —

LISTED by Duncumb (1805) as one of the more valuable old apples long grown in Herefordshire orchards, the variety is so named because when it is cut across the middle the carpel threads are seen as ten red spots in a circle around the core. Other varieties may show this feature, which has led to some confusion over names (see *Introduction 2*). Although listed as a cider variety, in later times TEN COMMANDMENTS may have been planted mainly as a novelty, for the nurseryman John Basham of Bassaleg reports in the Journal of the Royal Horticultural Society that he saw the variety for the first time in 1899 in an orchard at Cwmcarvan in Monmouthshire.

It is recorded in Gardeners' Chronicle (1877) that a party of members and guests of the Woolhope Club was shown this variety in an orchard at Breinton, near Hereford. Among the guests was Alice Blanche Ellis, artist for *The Herefordshire Pomona*, who spent the following day painting local apples and pears, so it is probably the Breinton apple that is shown in her watercolour of TEN COMMANDMENTS. However, her illustration was not included in the *Pomona* where the variety received only a passing mention in a list of 'Local Varieties of Cider Apples'.

TEN COMMANDMENTS was exhibited, as a dessert or cider apple, at the National Apple Congress at Chiswick in 1883, by the Cranston Nursery of Hereford. It was described in Hogg (1884). The apple is ripe in November.

Size	*Small-medium (52 × 48mm)*	Stalk	*Slender, usually projecting beyond base*
Shape	*Round-conical, with slight, uneven ribs and crowns*	Flesh	*White, usually suffused with red under the skin and along the coreline; tender, with an agreeable sub-acid flavour*
Skin	*Smooth, ground colour yellow, largely covered by dark, mahogany-red flush and dark red streaks*		
Lenticels	*Small, round, pale-brown, scarcely noticeable*	Tube	*Funnel-shaped (7–8mm); stamens marginal*
Basin	*Ribbed or puckered*	Core	*Basal, axile-closed, cells elliptical or round*
Eye	*Closed, sepals connivent, erect, with tips spreading or recurved*	Seeds	*Plump, shortly acute or apiculate (7mm)*
Cavity	*Regular, lined with fine brown russet, which may spread over base*	Flowers	*Pollination group 3 (13)*

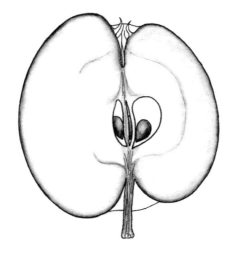

TEWKESBURY BARON

Mid-season dessert

THIS attractive brightly coloured fruit is similar in general appearance to a large DEVONSHIRE QUARRENDEN, but has an insipid flavour. A Gloucestershire apple, presumably originating in the Tewkesbury area, the variety appears to have been exhibited first by J. C. Wheeler and Sons of Gloucester, at the National Apple Congress held at Chiswick in 1883. In his report of the Congress for the Royal Horticultural Society, Barron (1884) describes it as "specially attractive, though of inferior quality". It was exhibited as a cider or culinary apple. Although illustrated for *The Herefordshire Pomona*, TEWKESBURY BARON was not included in the published work.

Size	Medium, but variable, (65 × 54mm)		Cavity	Rather wide and deep, lined with greenish russet which may spread over base
Shape	Flat-round to flat-conical, larger fruit slightly ribbed, with low crowns		Stalk	Short, usually within cavity, slightly flared at tip
Skin	Smooth, greasy when ripe, pale green becoming yellow-green, almost completely covered by crimson flush and some red stripes		Flesh	White with greenish tinge, soft, fairly juicy, weak flavour
Lenticels	Round to oval, grey, conspicuous on yellow ground		Tube	Funnel-shaped, stamens median or marginal
Basin	Rather shallow, slightly ribbed, sometimes puckered or beaded		Core	Median or basal, axile-closed or open, cells broadly ovate or round
Eye	Medium sized, usually open, sepals erect with spreading tips		Seeds	Plump, acute (6–7mm)
			Flowers	Pollination group 2 (7)

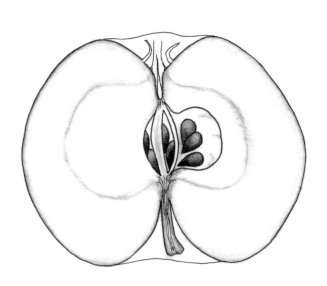
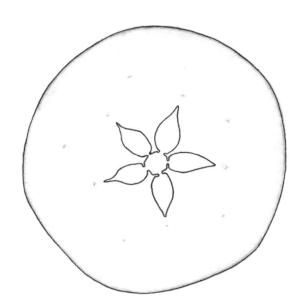

TILLINGTON COURT

— *Mid or late season culinary* —

TILLINGTON COURT is a triploid variety which will grow into a large spreading tree. Apples of this variety, sent from Herefordshire, were shown at the Crystal Palace exhibition of the Royal Horticultural Society in 1934. At that time Mr. H. Barnett, of Tilehurst in Berkshire, commented, "it is an apple I have long known as 'Tillington Court Pippin' the tradition at Tillington Court being that it was raised there many years ago". Taylor (1946) aptly describes its colouring as like that of TOM PUTT and writes that it was then being grown commercially at Tillington Court, which is situated five kilometres north-west of Hereford.

The large handsome cooker remains popular and local nurseries which grow it find a ready market. The apples are in season from October until January and cook to a deep yellow, fairly sharp and flavoursome purée.

Size	*Large or very large (84 × 74mm)*	Cavity	*Broad, deep, regular or lipped, sometimes lined by brownish russet*
Shape	*Oblong, somewhat flattened top and bottom, often with obvious ribs ending in prominent crowns, but sometimes fairly regular*	Stalk	*Stout, level with base or projecting, straight or slightly flared at tip*
Skin	*Smooth, waxy, background green becoming yellow, overlain with broad bright red stripes and a red flush (up to 95%)*	Flesh	*Cream, greenish around the core, soft, juicy, acidic*
		Tube	*Slightly funnel-shaped (7-10mm), stamens usually median, sometimes marginal*
Lenticels	*Round or oval, small, not conspicuous except when surrounded by pale areola*	Core	*Median, usually axile-closed, cells obovate or elliptical*
Basin	*Broad, deep, sometimes ribbed*	Seeds	*Plump, acute (8–9mm)*
Eye	*Fairly large, closed, sepals erect-convergent with reflexed tips*	Flowers	*Pollination group 4 (15)*

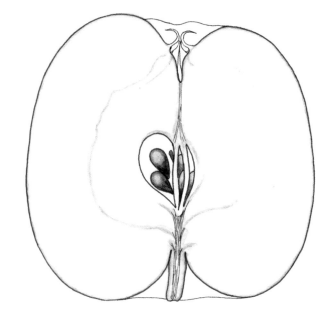
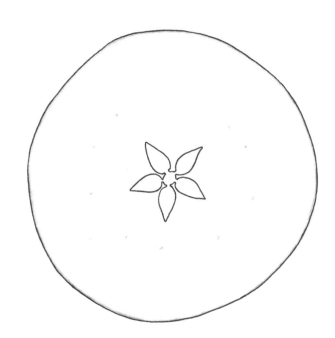

GLOSSARY

TERMS USED IN THE DESCRIPTION OF APPLE VARIETIES

EXTERNAL MORPHOLOGY OF FRUIT

Fig. 1 *External Morphology* (SEVERN BANK)

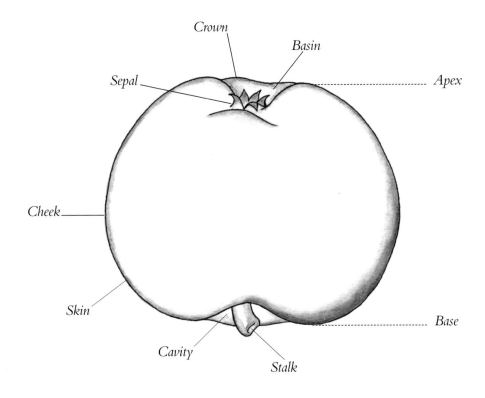

Fig. 2 *To show method of measuring*

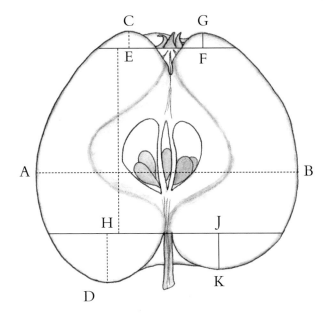

A *to* B =	Diameter
C *to* D =	Height
E *to* F =	Basin width
H *to* J =	Cavity width
$\dfrac{\text{C } to \text{ E} + \text{G } to \text{ F}}{2} =$	Basin depth
$\dfrac{\text{H } to \text{ D} + \text{J } to \text{ K}}{2} =$	Cavity depth

SIZE

The sizes given in the text are only a general guide. They are averages from measuring at least 15 apples, after discarding king fruits and the largest and smallest specimens. Sizes are quoted as diameter × height (mm). For details on measuring see *Fig. 2*. The specimens measured are taken from mature trees. If a tree bears a heavy crop the apples will tend to be smaller, and conversely young trees, especially on dwarfing root-stocks, tend to produce larger apples. Fruit size also varies according to soil type, drainage and weather conditions.

In categorising sizes, the diameter measurements are used.

Size category	Diameter (mm)
Very small	*Below 45*
Small	*45 – 54*
Small – medium	*55 – 59*
Medium	*60 – 69*
Medium – large	*70 – 74*
Large	*75 – 84*
Very large	*85 and above*

Fig. 3 *Apple shapes*

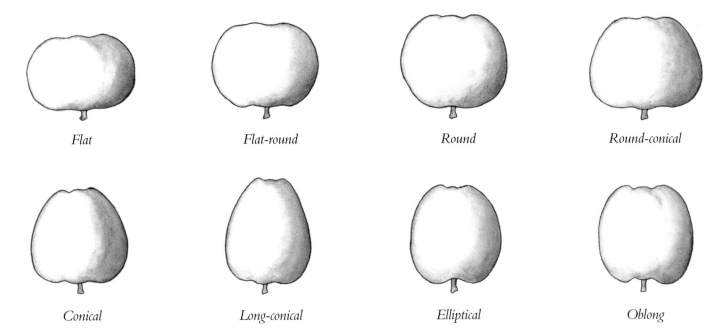

| *Flat* | *Flat-round* | *Round* | *Round-conical* |

| *Conical* | *Long-conical* | *Elliptical* | *Oblong* |

Regular	*Round in transverse section, without ribs/ridges/angles.*
Angular/ Ribbed	*With ridges/ribs, which may extend from base to apex and end as crowns. The degree of ribbing can best be seen in a transverse section.*
Crowns	*Up to five knobs which mark the end of ridges, at the apex around the eye.*
Skin Texture	*Described as smooth, rough, waxy, greasy or dry. Apples which feel waxy when picked, often become greasy in store. An apple with a russet skin or prominent lenticels feels rough.*
Bloom	*A whitish waxy layer over the surface of the skin, prominent in some red apples such as SPARTAN and MICHAELMAS RED. The bloom rubs off when an apple is handled.*
Scarf Skin	*A whitish or silvery layer of skin, particularly on the base of some varieties like LORD DERBY or ALFRISTON.*
Aroma	*The scent of an apple before it is cut.*
Ground Colour	*The underlying skin colour, normally starting green and becoming yellow or cream as the fruit ripens.*
Flush	*The ground colour is often partly or wholly covered by a more or less uniform layer of red. The extent is sometimes indicated in the text as a percentage.*
Stripes	*Narrow or broad streaks of red. Both flush and stripes tend to be more pronounced on the side of the fruit exposed to the sun.*
Russet	*Rough, brownish outer layer of skin, which may cover entire fruit or form a network (reticulate or netted russet) or be present as irregular patches, smudges or flecks. Most varieties have some russet in the cavity, where it is often present in concentric layers described as scaly russet. Varieties in which the russet cover is more or less complete are referred to as 'Russets' e.g. EGREMONT RUSSET. Varieties which have patchy russet and some exposed colour are known as 'Reinettes' e.g. COX'S ORANGE PIPPIN.*
Hair lines	*Narrow, raised lines which may extend from base to apex, are found in a proportion of apples of some cultivars e.g. ONIBURY PIPPIN.*
Lenticels	*Appear as dots on the skin and are pores which allow the exchange of gases between the external atmosphere and the living tissues inside the apple. The lenticels are usually smaller and more abundant near the top of the fruit. Their shape, size, distribution and prominence can be helpful in identification. Seen through a hand lens or magnifying glass lenticels may be round, oval, angular or stellate (star shaped) in outline. Their prominence depends on their size and degree of contrast with the skin ground colour.*
Areolæ	*Small circular patches of a different colour surrounding the lenticels of some cultivars.*
Basin	*A depression, of variable width and depth, around the eye. The sides may be smooth, ridged (if ribs on the side of the fruit extend into the basin), puckered or beaded. See Fig. 4.*
Eye	*After flowering the petals drop but the five sepals remain around the opening to the tube to form the eye. The eye is described as closed if the sepals meet to cover the aperture, or open if the sepals separate exposing the aperture.*
Sepal pose	*The size of the eye depends on the size of the sepals and their pose i.e. the angle and direction of their growth. The sepal pose is a useful identification aid. See Fig. 5.*
Cavity	*The depressed part around the stalk at the base. The cavity may be regular (even), ridged or lipped, i.e. with a bulge on one side which deflects the stalk.*
Stalk	*The length of the stalk and the shape of the tip are often rather variable features, but may sometimes aid identification. Short stalks are described as fleshy if they are surrounded by soft tissue. See Fig. 6.*

Fig. 4 *Types of basin*

| Smooth | Ridged | Puckered | Beaded |

Fig. 5 *Types of sepal pose*

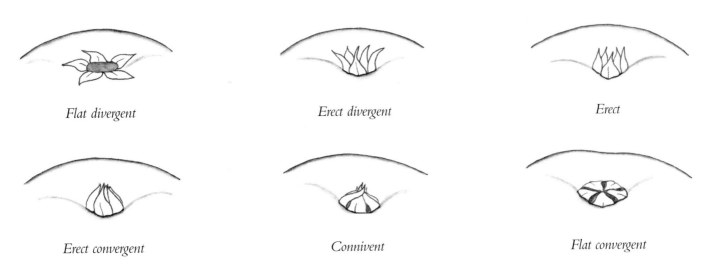

| Flat divergent | Erect divergent | Erect |

| Erect convergent | Connivent | Flat convergent |

Fig. 6 *Stalk tips*

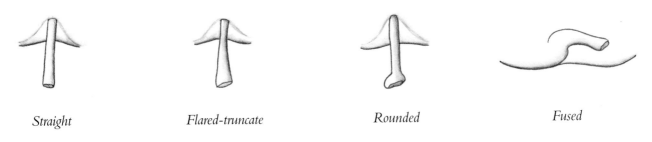

| Straight | Flared-truncate | Rounded | Fused |

INTERNAL ANATOMY OF FRUIT

Fig. 7 *Vertical (longitudinal) section of fruit*

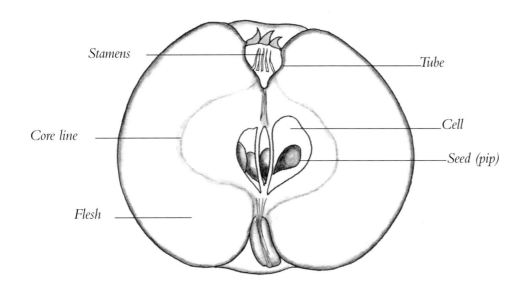

Stamens

Tube

Core line

Cell

Seed (pip)

Flesh

These features can be seen when a fruit is cut in half vertically, from the centre of the eye to the stalk, using a thin-bladed knife.

Symmetry	*If the two sides of the fruit are roughly equal, the fruit is described as symmetrical; if markedly unequal it is asymmetrical. See Fig. 8.*	Core line	*A cylinder of vascular tissue just outside the core, supplying the other parts of the flower. In a transverse section it may show up as distinct dots (red in* TEN COMMANDMENTS) *and there is sometimes a wavy line associated with it known as the Truelle line. The three positions in which the core line meets the tube can be seen in a longitudinal section, as seen in Fig. 11.*
Tube	*The tube below the eye may be conical or funnel-shaped*		
Stamens	*The three positions occupied by the stamens inside the tube are shown in Fig. 10.*		
Core	*The core normally consists of five carpels (cells) with tough horny walls, which contain the seeds.*	Cells	*The shape of the cells (carpels) as seen in longitudinal section is shown in Fig. 12.*
Core position	*The position of the core is described as (a) basal, if the core is closer to the stalk, (b) median, if it is mid-way between base and apex, or (c) proximal, if it is closer to the apex.*	Tufting	*In some cultivars e.g.,* NEWLAND SACK, *the inner surface of the cells has raised lines with a woolly covering known as tufting.*

Fig. 8 *Fruit symmetry*

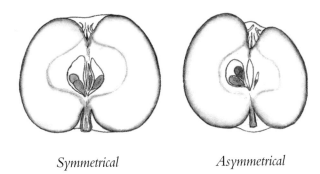

Symmetrical   Asymmetrical

Fig. 9 *Tube type*

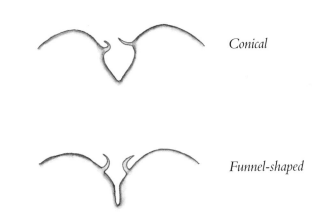

Conical

Funnel-shaped

Fig. 10

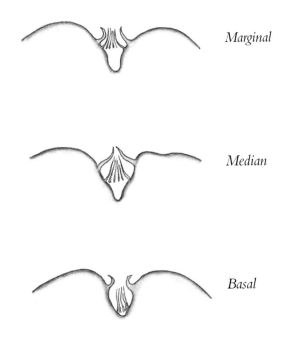

Marginal

Median

Basal

Fig. 11

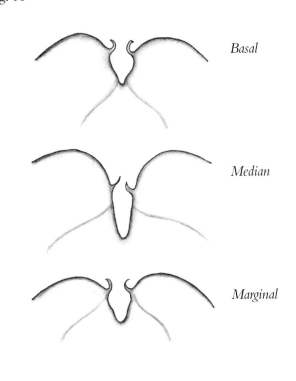

Basal

Median

Marginal

Fig. 12

Ovate   Elliptical   Round   Obovate

Axis — The arrangement of the cells in relation to the fruit axis can be seen in a transverse section cut through the widest part of the apple. The three possible arrangements are shown in Fig. 13.

Seeds (pips) — The four shapes noted are shown in Fig. 14.

Pollination — Without pollination there is little or no fruit set; few cultivars are self-fertile. For effective pollination apple trees need neighbours which flower at about the same time. Relative flowering times are indicated in a sequence of numbers, 1 being the earliest to flower. Most nursery catalogues classify the varieties they offer for sale into groups which flower within a few days of each other and thus provide suitable pollination partners.

Relative flowering times (pollination numbers) and pollinating groups are both indicated in the text e.g. FORESTER (pollination number 16, group 4) could be pollinated by PIG'S NOSE PIPPIN (14), ONIBURY PIPPIN (15), or any other cultivar in pollination group 4 except triploid varieties, which produce little fertile pollen.

Triploid — Triploid varieties e.g. TILLINGTON COURT, have an extra set of chromosomes in each cell and usually produce large vigorous trees but they do need two other varieties which flower at the same time to provide effective pollination.

Fruit maturity — The period when fruit of a variety is good to eat, or fit to be cooked, is noted by months. To provide a sharper flavour cookers are often used before the fruit is fully ripe. Early and mid-season cultivars cannot usually be stored for more than a short time. Late cultivars should be picked by mid-October and are then stored until fully ripe.

Fruit position — There are three categories describing the places where flower/fruit buds, and subsequent fruits, are produced in a particular cultivar. The fruit position will affect the type of pruning required.

(a) Tip bearers — The fruit buds develop in a cluster at the tip of stems produced during the current season.

(b) Spur bearers — Fruit is produced on very short side branches (spurs) on stems which are at least two years old.

(c) Partial tip bearers — Fruit is produced partly on spurs on older stems and partly at the tips of the current year's stems.

Fig. 13

Axile closed

Axile open

Abaxile

Fig. 14

 Acute

 Acuminate

 Blunt

 Apiculate

Vegetative Features

Leaves
Leaf features such as the size and shape of the lamina (leaf blade), the relative length of the petiole (leaf stalk) and the size and shape of the stipules may be additional features helpful in identification, but vegetative features generally show a greater degree of variation than reproductive characters and hence are less reliable.

Leaf margin
The main forms of indentation of the leaf margin are shown in Fig. 16.

Fig. 15 *Features of leaves*

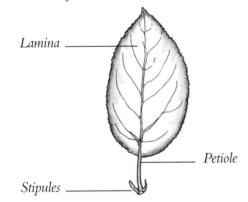

Lamina

Petiole

Stipules

Fig. 16

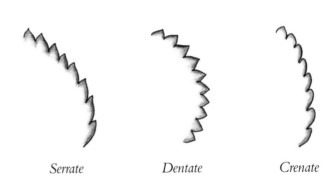

Serrate   Dentate   Crenate

One leaf of each variety described in *Welsh Marches Pomona,* taken from a mid-stem position on a new shoot in mid-summer, is illustrated on the following pages. Leaves from this position appear to be rather less variable than those found on short side branches (spurs). Other features such as the folding of the leaves and the density of the hairs on the lower surface of the lamina may also be useful pointers to the identification of a variety.

SCALE:

Leaves are drawn × ¼ life size; details of margins are drawn × 1

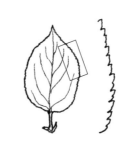

BRIDSTOW WASP

BRINGEWOOD PIPPIN

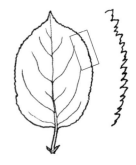

BRITHMAWR

BROOKES'S

BYFORD WONDER

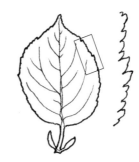

CHATLEY KERNEL

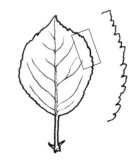

CISSY

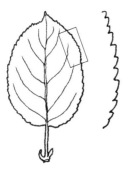

COLWALL
QUOINING

CREDENHILL PIPPIN

FORESTER

GREEN PURNELL

HUNT'S DUKE
OF GLOUCESTER

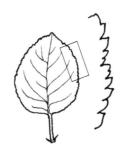

KING COFFEE

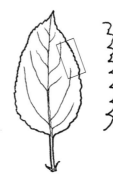

KING'S ACRE
BOUNTIFUL

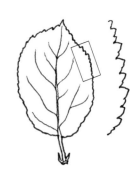

LANDORE

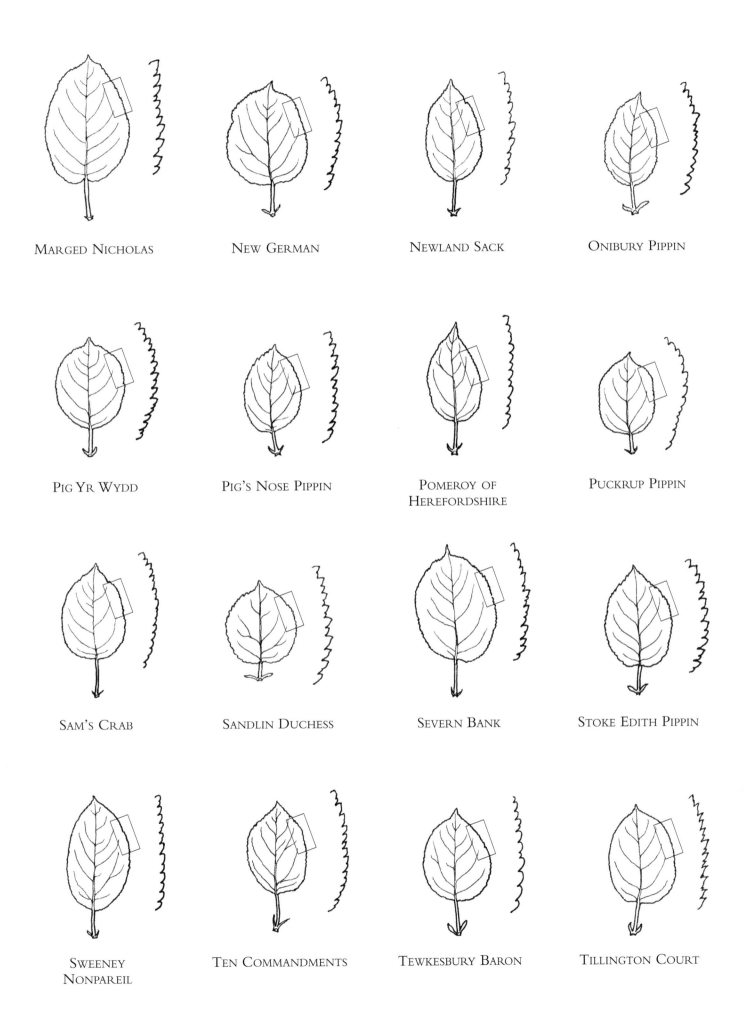

MARGED NICHOLAS

NEW GERMAN

NEWLAND SACK

ONIBURY PIPPIN

PIG YR WYDD

PIG'S NOSE PIPPIN

POMEROY OF
HEREFORDSHIRE

PUCKRUP PIPPIN

SAM'S CRAB

SANDLIN DUCHESS

SEVERN BANK

STOKE EDITH PIPPIN

SWEENEY
NONPAREIL

TEN COMMANDMENTS

TEWKESBURY BARON

TILLINGTON COURT

BIBLIOGRAPHY

Bannister, Rev. A.T.	*The History of Ewias Harold,* 1902
Barron, A.F.,	*British Apples,* 1884
Bultitude, J., 1979	*Index of the Apple Collection at the National Fruit Trials,* 1979
Bultitude, J.	*A Guide to the Identification of International Varieties,* 1983
Bunyard, E. A.	*A Handbook of Hardy Fruits more commonly grown in Great Britain: Apples and Pears,* 1920
Bunyard, G. & O. Thomas	*The Fruit Garden,* 1906
Chittenden, F. J. (Ed.)	*Apples and Pears: Varieties and cultivation in 1934 (Report of RHS Conference),* 1935
Copas, L.	*A Somerset Pomona: The Cider Apples of Somerset,* 2001
Davies, J.	*A History of Wales,* 1993
Dew, Rev. E.N.(Ed)	*Extracts from the Cathedral Registers, Hereford, AD 1275–1535,* 1932
Duncumb, J.	*General View of the Agriculture of the County of Hereford,* 1805
Durham, H. E.	*The Recognition of Fruit in Journal of Pomology Vol. 1,* 1919-20
Evelyn, J.	*Sylva... Pomona: or, an Appendix Concerning Fruit-Trees in Relation to Cider...,* 1664
Fox, C. & Lord Raglan	*Monmouthshire Houses,* 1951-54
Gerard, J.	*The Herball or General Historie of Plantes,* 1597
Hogg, R.	*British Pomology,* 1850
Hogg, R.	*The Fruit Manual, Edition IV,* 1875
Hogg, R.	*The Fruit Manual, Edition V,* 1884
Hogg, R. & H. G. Bull	*The Herefordshire Pomona,* 1876-85
Hogg, R. & H. G. Bull	*The Apple and Pear as Vintage Fruits,* 1886
Hooker, W.	*Pomona Londinensis Vol. I,* 1818
Janson, H. F.	*Pomona's Harvest,* 1996
Johnson, Richard	*Survey of the Crickhowell and Tretower estates of the Earl of Worcester (Badminton Vol 3),* 1587
Juniper, B.E.& D.J.Mabberley	*The Story of the Apple,* 2006
Knight, T.A.	*Pomona Herefordiensis,* 1811
Lawson, W.	*A New Orchard and Garden...,* 1618
Lindley, G.	*Guide to the Orchard and Kitchen Garden,* 1831
Lindley, J.	*The Pomological Magazine,* 1828-30

Linnard, W.	*Welsh Woods and Forests: History and Utilization, 1982*
Marcher Apple Network	*Apples of the Welsh Marches, 2002*
Morgan, J. and A. Richards	*The Book of Apples, 1993*
Morganwg, I	*Welsh Names of Apples in The Cambrian Journal III, 1858*
Parkinson, J.	*Paradisi in Sole Paradisus Terrestris, 1629*
Plomer, W. (Ed.)	*Kilvert's Diary: Selections from the diary of the Rev. Francis Kilvert, 1960*
Pughe, O.	*A National Dictionary of the Welsh Language, 1873*
Radford, C.A.R.	*Tretower: The Castle and Court in Brycheiniog VI, 1960*
Ronalds, H.	*Pyrus Malus Brentfordiensis, 1831*
Sanders, R.	*The English Apple, 1988*
Scott, J.	*The Orchardist, 1873*
Smith, M.W.G.	*National Apple Register of the United Kingdom, 1971*
Taylor, H.V.	*The Apples of England, 1946*
Thompson, R.	*Gardener's Assistant, 1853*
Whiting, F.	*Mss. Notebook of varieties of fruit cultivated at Credenhill, 1895-1906*
Williams, R.R.	*Bulmer's Pomona, 1987*

OTHER SOURCES

1350-1650	*Badminton Estate Papers, National Library of Wales*
Early 19th century	*Estate papers of Doldowlod, Rads., Sweeney Hall, Shropshire*
1800-1954	*Transactions, Proceedings, Journals and Reports of the Royal Horticultural Society*
1841 ff	*Gardeners Chronicle*
circa 1870	*Catalogues of J. C. Wheeler and Sons, Gloucester*
1870-1885	*Transactions of the Woolhope Naturalists' Field Club*
1875-1884	*Unpublished watercolour illustrations painted for* The Herefordshire Pomona
1880-1907	*Catalogues of Richard Smith and Co., Worcester*
1883	*Archaeologia Cambrensis Vol XIV (Priory Charters)*
1919-1931	*Catalogues of King's Acre Nurseries, Hereford*
1995 ff	*Newsletters and Reports of the Marcher Apple Network*

PATRONS, SPONSORS & SUBSCRIBERS

THE MARCHER APPLE NETWORK IS GRATEFUL FOR THE SUPPORT OF THOSE LISTED BELOW
WHOSE GENEROSITY CONTRIBUTED SUBSTANTIALLY TO THE PRODUCTION OF THIS BOOK

PATRONS

Lawrence & Elizabeth Banks

Ray & Norma Boddington

& one anonymous Patron

SPONSORS

Peter & Vicky Austerfield

Gillian Barter

Sir Brooke Boothby

Jim Chapman

Geoffrey Crofts

D. H. Ferguson-Thomas

Tom Froggatt

Dr. & Mrs. John N. Gibbs

William Gibbs

Kemerton Conservation Trust

*The Revd. Michael
& Dr. Lesley Kneen*

Daphne Lush

*Frank P. Matthews Ltd.,
Trees for Life*

Gareth Martyn Pugh

Mr. Clive Richards OBE DL

Graham Sprackling

Brian M. Stephens

J. & J. Tennent

Annie Wood & Brendan Sheehy

& one anonymous Sponsor

SUBSCRIBERS

Apocalypse Cider – Chris Horn

C. Attfield

Jemima & Lola Austerfield

David Barker

Barlow and Loveday

Paul Barnett Trees

Linda Blenkinship

Christopher Boddington

Mr. & Mrs. Boutle

*The British Columbia
Fruit Testers Association*

Christine Cleaton

Paul & Sandi Evans

Glenn Facer

Brian Fox

Mr. & Mrs. Colin Gardiner

Richard Hancock

Ian Harrison

Martin Hewitt

Bernard & Wendy Hill

Mrs. H. T. Hillier

Christopher & Margaret Jenkins

Sheila I. Leitch

Anthony J. Malpas

J. C. Morgan

Dr. Joan Morgan

Robin & Sylvia O'Brien

Tim Porter

Jon Porter

Robin Porter

Lt. Colonel & Mrs. T. B. d'E Powell

Prof. Martin & Mrs Pamela Redwood

John & Felicity Rogers

Sarah Sankey-Barker

John Savidge

Kathryn & Paul Silk

David H. T. Smith

On behalf of Arlo & Daisy Stark

Shelly & Mike Stroud

Helen Thomas

H. Weston & Sons Ltd.

Richard Wheeler

Roger Williams MP

& three anonymous Subsribers

THE MARCHER
APPLE NETWORK

THE Marcher Apple Network (MAN) was set up in 1993 to promote interest in local fruit and traditional orchards. MAN is now a registered charity and a company limited by guarantee with about 300 members. To further its aims, MAN mounts displays of local varieties of apples and pears at many countryside shows, provides advice on orchard management, publishes and sells relevant literature, holds identification sessions and organises training courses for developing skills such as pruning and grafting.

By arrangement with landowners in the region, MAN maintains five 'Museum Orchards' where unidentified apples can be grown alongside known local varieties. Where possible our orchards are managed in a traditional way to favour biodiversity and foster the biological control of pests and diseases. Recently MAN has been very fortunate to be given the new Paramor Orchard in Powys, where all the apples described in *Welsh Marches Pomona* will be cultivated.

Special events are arranged to celebrate our orchard heritage and members are encouraged to take part in the management of the orchards and other activities, such as guided visits to nurseries. A regular news sheet and the annually published magazine, *Apples and Pears,* keep members informed about events.